MARK,

You ARE ONE OF MY
FAVORITE PEOPLE ON THE
PLANET! WE'VE HAD SOME
FUN TIMES AND SHARED
A LOT OF LAUGHTER.
THAT'S WHAT LIFE IS ALL
ABOUT.

ENJOY THE
BOOK

Doug

FIFTY
SHADES
of
TRUE
CRIME

SEX, DRUGS, AND KILLER KINK

BY
DOUGLAS FIFER

ISBN: 978-1-964934-07-5

Printed in the United States of America

This book is dedicated to the men and women of law enforcement who keep our communities safe. It's not an easy job, but anything worthwhile rarely is. If you see a police officer, thank them for their service, as this small act of kindness is always appreciated. A portion of book sales will be donated to organizations supporting families of fallen law enforcement officers.[1]

---

[1] While sayings, quotes, and details have been condensed, they may not be exact word-for-word translations but are factually derived from direct involvement, criminal complaints, and case reports. Where appropriate, names have been changed out of respect for the families.

TABLE OF CONTENTS

INTRODUCTION

**Everything in this book is about sex,
except sex—which is about power.**

Cucumbers, cough drops, pizza, or pigs—which one would you use for fucking? Before you say, "Uh . . . none," I can all but guarantee that by the end of this book, you'll consider at least one of them. What's more, you will soon find out who uses them all. This true crime thriller with a sexual twist will be a reading adventure unlike any other. While most of these police investigations resulted in criminal charges, a few went far beyond the price of prison. You'll be entertained, sickened, and awestruck along the way. Each of us has different sexual boundaries, so what are the limits of kink in your sex life? It's time to discover that just fucking with the lights on isn't so naughty—but how and what you fuck can be.

The naked truth that lies ahead is meant to expose how even "normal" people might have disturbing, illegal, or even deadly kinks. We've all struggled with unfulfilled sexual curiosity, trying to reconcile those desires with what's considered ordinary in real life. People are biologically hardwired for—sometimes insanely driven by—sex, and the crime stories in this book demonstrate that. They are as raw and unfiltered as it gets. Inhibitions and unfamiliarity can cramp your style when it comes to pushing the limits, but within these pages, you just might find your new level of freak. We'll cover everything from mild fetishes to extreme kinks that may shock you to your core. I'll warn you: it won't be easy, and getting there requires visits to sexual heaven and sexual hell. You'll find yourself confessing to those desires while reading this book—maybe not out loud, but either way, you won't be able to silence that inner voice.

The person who'll lead you on this journey to sexual utopia isn't who you expected. It's not a sex therapist, your doctor, or even your partner. It's (surprise, surprise!) a cop from Alaska, and I'll be sharing stories from a career filled with the good, the bad, and the ugly. Why, you might ask, should I listen to a cop about sex? Well, for starters, I've used a cough drop or two during intimate encounters. We'll get to the relative innocence of this admission later, but more importantly, I've witnessed firsthand some of the most shocking sexual acts you can imagine—so perverse, they simply defy belief. While Alaska offers undeniable beauty, it's also one of the coldest and darkest places on earth. The Last Frontier's unsavory side will be on full display as these bone-chilling accounts prove that beauty and desire are in the eye of the beholder. This will be a sobering look into the savage sexual lust that potentially lurks within us all. Most of us can manage those desires without acting on them, but others cannot resist.

If you blush at the mere thought of sex, or consider missionary position erotic, I'll be honest—this book may not be for you. But if you sometimes question whether your sex life is normal or wonder how far you'd go to spice things up, your personal polygraph awaits within these pages, and the truth *will* set you free. A bit of advice before we start, however: get ready for some emotionally dark humor. Laughter is the best medicine, and— take it from a cop—it will help keep your sanity in check. With that in mind, are you up for getting virtually fucked without any physical contact other than turning a page? Relax—it will be surprisingly cleansing, and you just might learn a thing or two.

CHAPTER ONE

NAME THAT CRIME

I cebreakers are a great way to help people ease into difficult topics of discussion. They allow us to connect and feel less guarded. For that reason, consider this a warmup chapter that requires your participation. While the flavor of this book is purely sex, the subsequent chapters increase in intensity and evolve into more traditional storylines. This isn't for the faint of heart. You're about to get mentally twisted reading this, but I have a trade-off that just might make it worthwhile. Want to be the life of the party, be the center of attention, and always leave a lasting impression? I mean, why the hell not? And guess what? You don't need to be charismatic, famous, or funny to achieve this, but you will need a few interesting stories. As luck would have it, I've got your back. The following real-life cases aren't just attention grabbers; they are jaw-droppers. Be forewarned: prepare yourself for an interactive reading experience that will challenge the moral fabric of our society.

According to a 2023 Gallup poll, Americans say U.S. moral values are not good and getting worse. Remarkably, 54 percent of respondents currently rate our values as being poor. On top of that, 83 percent believe our moral standards are declining. This chapter will require engaging this dilemma with your eyes wide open.[2] Morality is a human biological attribute, and we are generally predisposed to judge good and evil; however, moral codes vary from person to person. In the 1800s, Charles Darwin wrote about the moral sense, which, according to him, emerges from the foundation of instinct and impulse in all human beings. He believed the standard of morality improves as humanity evolves and gets smarter. So how are we doing roughly two hundred years later? Sorry, Charlie, but we're fucked!

Name That Crime is exactly as it sounds. It's your chance to play cop, detective, and FBI profiler. Just like in the good old days of the Wild West, I'm deputizing you to help solve these crimes. If you think the following incidents couldn't happen in today's world, think again. Many states still have laws allowing police officers to deputize civilians, so repeat after me:

Law Enforcement Oath of Honor

On my honor, I will never betray my badge, my integrity, my character, or the public trust.

I will always have the courage to hold myself and others accountable for our actions.

I will uphold the constitution, my community, and the agency I serve.

---

[2] *Moral Issues*, (Gallup, 2023). https://news.gallup.com/poll/1681/moral-issues.aspx. Article also viewable at: dougfifer.com.

Congratulations, you're now the new sheriff in town. The following cases will describe graphic criminal behavior. As the reader, you will be given several options as to what unlawful act the individual committed. Study the mug shot, analyze crime scene photos, and review the criminal laws before selecting which offense you would charge.

You are now the crime fighter—so . . . Name That Crime.

Man's Best Friend . . .

(Booking photo)

You've seen the mug shot. Now it's time to pick the perversion:

1. **Indecent Exposure.** According to Alaska Statute 11.41.460, "an offender commits the crime of indecent exposure in the second degree if the offender knowingly exposes the offender's genitals in the presence of another person with reckless disregard for the offensive, insulting, or frightening effect the act may have."

2. **Criminal Mischief.** According to Alaska Statute 11.46.486, "a person commits the crime of criminal mischief in the fifth degree if, having no right to do so or any

reasonable ground to believe the person has such a right, with reckless disregard for the risk of harm to or loss of the property or with intent to cause substantial inconvenience to another, the person tampers with the property of another."

3. **Failure to Register as a Sex Offender or Child Kidnapper.** According to Alaska Statute 11.56.840, "a person commits the crime of failure to register as a sex offender or child kidnapper in the second degree if the person is required to register under AS 12.63.010 (related to the registration of sex offenders)."

Okay, looking at the mug shot, at first glance, this is actor Matt Damon's doppelgänger. Hopefully, that's where the similarities end. Now, because of the nature of his crimes, bagging this bad guy might get a little emotionally painful for you. This sadistic bastard is going to rub you the wrong way; he is 100 percent going to make your blood boil. The incident in question takes place in the small village of Klawock, Alaska, a community of around nine hundred residents located near Ketchikan. As a side note, this is where my family is from. And no, thank God, he's not our black sheep. The area boasts some of the most pristine and picturesque land Mother Earth has to offer. But on this day, that majestic beauty would become tainted with a disgusting and vile act.

Let's set the stage: imagine yourself enjoying a beautiful Alaskan spring day. The sun is out, birds are chirping, and it's finally time to take Fido to the local dog park. After a harsh Alaskan winter, it's a great place for community friends to gather and let their pups socialize. Max is running free, Duke is sniffing every dog's ass, and Bella is rolling in the grass. In 2008, this was a tail-wagging utopia—until it wasn't. What changed?

This one's going to be hard to ease into, so I'll just cut to the chase. You see, on this day, man's best friend literally got fucked . . . by a man.

Say it isn't so! Oh, it is so, and it gets worse. Harold Simpson, a twenty-six-year-old, not only fucked one unsuspecting pooch but also went back-to-back with another. So how was this dog rapist caught? A local resident witnessed him pulling a golden retriever into the woods after lassoing it with a green rope. She thought it odd when the dog was noticeably reluctant to go with him. Twenty minutes later, the retriever reappeared and, soon after, so did Harold Simpson. He then targeted a black lab, using the same green rope to drag it into the woods. The woman decided to seek help and asked two local men to check on the lab.

What did those two men find in the woods? They found Harold Simpson in the act of sexually assaulting the lab. He had tied the poor pup to a tree with the rope and duct-taped the snout shut and was sodomizing it. Remember the earlier guarantee of your blood boiling? No ifs, ands, or buts about it, we should lock this perverted son of a bitch up and throw away the key. But wait—as you probably noticed by now, the criminal statutes above don't seem to fit this crime. It's because in 2008, loving on Lassie was *not* a crime. Let that sink in for a moment: dog fucking was legal! The best cops could do was charge Harold Simpson with two counts of misdemeanor criminal mischief, specifically defined as tampering with the property of another (in this case the dog owners'). The state-charging document read in part:

STATE OF ALASKA,

Plaintiff,

v.

HAROLD JAY SIMPSON,

Defendant.

In the First Judicial District, State of Alaska, HAROLD JAY SIMPSON, having no right to do so or any reasonable ground to believe he had such a right, did unlawfully tamper with the property of another with reckless disregard for the risk of harm to or loss of the property or with intent to cause substantial inconvenience to another. (Count I and Count II were identical.)

Do you read anything here that indicates we're dealing with a serial dog rapist? Nope, that's it. Two very minor charges that typically receive nothing but a slap on the wrist. Harold Simpson had premeditated these cruel assaults before ever arriving at the dog park. He brought a rope and tape and even took the time to handpick his victims from dozens of dogs. In the end, none of this mattered because Harold Simpson could not face more serious charges. He got off scot-free for literally screwing the pooch. Although a bit late in the case of Mr. Simpson, we have since enacted a law (Alaska Statute 11.61.140), which directly prohibits engaging in sexual conduct with animals.

Cool as a Cucumber . . .

Pet lovers, you probably need to recharge your batteries after that emotional roller coaster, and I don't blame you one bit. As luck would have it, the next crime on the police blotter is a bit more tranquil. The long summer days in Alaska are what residents live for; after being pent up for eight long months of hellish winter, it's time to enjoy the great outdoors. Most parts of the country enjoy four seasons, but Alaskans have only two—we place the rarely seen spring and fall into the honorable mention category. The following is an easily understood timeline of seasonal duration as well as a glimpse into the typical Alaskan's thought process throughout the year:

Fall: two weeks ("Winter is coming . . .")

Winter: eight months ("Just waiting for summer . . .")

Spring: two weeks ("Still waiting for summer . . .")

Summer: three months ("Time to get outside and party like there's no tomorrow . . .")

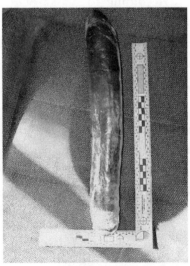

(Police photo)

Nothing screams "party in your pants" like the following story because, as you can see in the crime scene photo, there she is in all her glory. The ruler measuring it is a fractional L-shaped scale for forensic photography. It's six inches by twelve inches and is an absolute necessity when processing crime scenes. Oh, wait—you couldn't care less about the cool police ruler. You want to know more about the cucumber, but you've got work to do first. So . . . Name That Crime.

1. **Misconduct Involving a Corpse.** According to Alaska Statute 11.61.130, "a person commits the crime of misconduct involving a corpse if, except as authorized by law or in an emergency, the person intentionally disinters, removes, conceals, or mutilates a corpse; the person engages in sexual penetration of a corpse; or the person detains a corpse for debt or demand or upon a lien or charge."

2. **Prostitution.** According to Alaska Statute 11.66.100, "a person commits the crime of prostitution if the person engages in or agrees or offers to engage in sexual conduct in return for a fee; or offers a fee in return for sexual conduct."

3. **Driving Under the Influence (DUI).** According to Alaska Statute 28.35.030, "a person commits the crime of driving while under the influence of an alcoholic beverage, inhalant, or controlled substance if the person operates or drives a motor vehicle or operates an aircraft or watercraft while under the influence of an alcoholic beverage, intoxicating liquor, inhalant, or any controlled substance, singly or in combination."

Picture the quintessential "soccer mom" minivan riding dirty around the streets of Anchorage while the driver enjoys a few libations along the way. Summer outings in the late evening are common for Alaskans. Contrary to the darkness of winter, on the day of summer solstice, Anchorage gets a whopping twenty-two hours of sunlight. To help avoid cabin fever, chauffeuring yourself around town just to get out is a favorite pastime. But as we all know, driving hammered will get you nailed. If you somehow picked DUI, well, to the victor go the spoils.

Let's fast-forward to around 5:00 the next morning. I received a call from an officer working the night shift who excitedly told me, "You're not gonna believe this one!" While sharing is caring, the boys in blue at the Anchorage Police Department live by a code that states if you wake an officer up at the crack of dawn, *it better be good*. Oh, boy, was it ever.

The sequence of events went a little something like this: My coworker witnessed a red minivan swerving between lanes around midnight. Since there was a good chance the driver was impaired, a traffic stop was made. The minivan slowly pulled over to a stop. After the officer walked up to the driver's side, he tapped on the window. When it rolled down, he immediately smelled the odor of alcohol. The passenger side was littered with empty beer cans, and the driver was indifferently carefree enough to still have a fresh one in hand. He was completely oblivious to the seriousness of the situation; cops call this "too drunk to care." After a little incoherent chitchat, it was time for the field sobriety tests. The male suspect was told to step out of the vehicle, and he willingly attempted to do that. But unbeknownst to all involved, the minivan had not been placed into the park position. The driver had been pressing the brake with his foot, so when he tried to get out of the vehicle, it started rolling.

In fairness, the guy tried desperately to place the shifter into park. Being three sheets to the wind made this small task impossible. The minivan was on a slight decline and was now gaining speed. By this time, the officer was jogging next to it while leaning inside trying to grab the parking brake. Before he lost his footing, and without any other options, he pulled the male through the open window. Both fell backward onto the roadway with the guy on top of him. As uncomfortable as this seems, the best is yet to come. The man's pants had come off at some point during the struggle, and he wasn't wearing any underwear.

The officer quickly rolled him off. Having a bare ass touching you, with the potential of penis contact, is one hell of a motivator. But that was the least of his problems; an unwanted friend called "fecal matter" had made an appearance. We're not talking a little shart from an accidental fart—this was full-blown diarrhea. The officer's pants, shirt, and boots, along with his hands and arms, were covered in poop. And to make matters worse, the drunk driver, who was also awash in his own feces, would still need to be criminally processed. During these special policing moments, officers may recall the very fitting Southwest Airlines slogan: "Wanna get away?"

After hearing the details of this true-blue shitshow, I let the officer know it didn't quite rise to the level of a 5:00 a.m. wakeup call. Perhaps a lunchtime setting would be easier on the sleep cycle since we were only talking about getting covered in poop. (If you are thinking food and revolting stories like this don't mix, keep in mind that cops share pretty much everything during their midday meals without missing a bite.) Before I had a chance to hang up with him, he said, "Wait. That's not the best part."

The runaway minivan had eventually crashed into a nearby ditch. The officer made a beeline for it in an attempt to retrieve the half-naked man's pants. The drunk guy was probably too far gone to care, but most cops are strongly opposed to free-swinging dicks while on duty. When the officer looked inside the van, he couldn't believe his eyes. A monstrosity lay on the driver's seat. By now, you probably have a good idea where this is going. Yes, the cucumber was up the guy's ass. As he was pulled through the window, his pants came off and the cucumber came out.

The medical term "fecal incontinence" has hopefully never been on your radar until now. It is usually caused by muscle and nerve damage for a variety of reasons, one being the "loss of stretch" in the rectum. Apparently, giant inserted fruits or vegetables can contribute to this unfortunate medical condition. But before we start judging, let's keep in mind that the American Heart Association does recommend four to five servings of fruits and vegetables per day.

Okay, hands down, this was now worthy of an any time call. I could be at my kid's baptism, and I would interrupt the priest to hear this shit sandwich. It was solid stuff, but I did have some follow-up questions for my fellow brother in blue.

"How big was the cucumber?" I asked.

"It was fucking massive," he said. "Like a foot long."

"Shut up! No chance it was that big."

"It was not only long, but it was thick too."

"Did you get a picture of it?"

"Seriously? I was covered from head to toe in crap! No, I didn't get a picture of it."

"Where is the cucumber now?"

"It's still in the minivan. I wasn't touching it."

"Where's the minivan?"

"It was impounded."

"Sounds like a hell of a night. You'd better go get your-self cleaned up."

The phone call may have ended, but I was left wanting more information. I needed to know the unknown: exactly how large was this beast? I called our dispatch center and asked them to pull up the call. They gave me the address of where the van was impounded. In my career, I've arrested murder-ers, negotiated with serial killers, and saved countless lives. With all of that being said, it's the little things I'm most proud of. This critically important cucumber investigation—getting to the truth of the matter—is what police work is all about. Upon grabbing my much-needed morning coffee, I was off to the tow yard.

After sweet-talking the receptionist with some *quote, unquote*, official business, I had the vehicle's key in hand, and I headed to the assigned space number. When I saw the mini-van, I remember being overly excited for what was to come. It was like Christmas when I was a kid, when I couldn't wait to open those presents. I placed the key into the driver's door and slowly but surely opened it. I was thinking to myself, *Wait for it . . . wait for it.* Let me tell you something and set the record straight: it was the largest cucumber I had ever laid eyes on. It was so enormous, I figured I must have misunderstood my fel-low officer when he had said, "It was all the way up there." This couldn't possibly fit into a human's ass, and if it could, I'd have assumed the investigation would have had to shift from a DUI to an official probe into death by cucumber.

Upon closer inspection, I noticed the cucumber was covered in clear plastic wrap. Before I tell you about the next discovery, let's change the name to "poo-cumber." With shit stuck on both ends, my investigation determined it had, in fact, been fully inserted. The nerdish police ruler described earlier shows the poo-cumber reaching an awe-inspiring fourteen inches in length, with more than two inches of girth. The suspect was only five feet, six inches tall and weighed 130 pounds. I guess it's true: big things do come in small packages.

What about the plastic wrap? Nothing special here; it's the simplest way to keep inserted fruits and vegetables clean. A quick unwrap takes it back to its original condition—salad, anyone?

I thought it would be respectful to thank my colleague for this little gem of a story by creating a calendar memorializing the event. It was appropriately titled "Cool as a Cucumber." Each month displayed an image reminding him of that fateful night. June featured the suspect's booking photo; July had the red minivan; August showed the peeled-off poop pants; September displayed the photo shown above; and on and on. Busting balls is therapy for cops.

I think it goes without saying your next encounter with a minivan might conjure something a bit mentally awkward. You'll look twice at the driver while wondering, "Did they just leave Sunday Mass, or perhaps do they have a fourteen-inch cucumber up their ass?"

A Germaphobe's Worst Nightmare . . .

Ever had someone cough or sneeze on you? It's a damned gross feeling. If you're thinking, *That's never happened to me*, sorry, but here's why you are in denial: a cough can travel at fifty miles per hour, with a sneeze reaching one hundred miles per hour while spraying out upwards of one hundred thousand droplets. Wondering what's the safe zone to avoid snot rockets? Let's just say, if you happen to be in the same room, you're doomed.

The Massachusetts Institute of Technology conducted a study on this very subject. Dr. Lydia Bourouiba, an associate professor specializing in fluid dynamics, noted in her research, "Droplets can travel the dimensions of a room and land up to six meters to eight meters away." I'll do the meter math for my fellow Americans: twenty-seven feet is one hell of an achoo!

Without digressing into human fluids too much, it must be said before we move on that cops are exposed to them all. Blood, not surprisingly, is one of the most common; we go to violent calls where people are often injured. Saliva, unfortunately, comes frequently from criminals who love to spit. Snot, mucus, and phlegm are never-ending and freely donated, and there's a lot of giving people out there. As for urine, I can't tell you how many people we deal with piss themselves. What about feces? Oh, yeah, more times than I can count. My favorite moment was patting down a suspect, feeling around their inner waistband for weapons, and coming out with shit on my hands. Now, while my personal hygiene may not be perfect, I can guarantee I don't have a pile of poop six inches above my ass crack. As you might have guessed, fecal matter is by far my least favorite human discharge. But all the shit in the world doesn't compare to the following 911 call.

Coprophobia is the fear of feces, but you've got a new phobia to discover, so . . . Name That Crime.

(Police photo)

1. **Assault.** According to Alaska Statute 11.41.230, "a person commits the crime of assault in the fourth degree if that person recklessly causes physical injury to another person."

2. **Harassment.** According to Alaska Statute 11.61.118, "a person commits the crime of harassment in the first degree if, under circumstances not proscribed under AS 11.41.434–11.41.440 (related to offenses against a minor), the person violates AS 11.61.120(a)(5) (related to harassment in the second degree) and the offensive physical contact is contact with human or animal blood, mucus, saliva, semen, urine, vomitus, or feces; or by the person touching through clothing another person's genitals, buttocks, or female breast."

3. **Indecent Exposure.** According to Alaska Statute 11.41.460, "an offender commits the crime of indecent exposure in the second degree if the offender knowingly exposes the offender's genitals in the presence of another person with reckless

disregard for the offensive, insulting, or frightening effect the act may have."

One of our officers responded with lights and sirens to a mental health facility located in the heart of Anchorage. A rather large male patient had pummeled numerous staff members and was roaming free in a common area. Several of the employees had been knocked out and remained unconscious on the floor. The officer, fearing for their safety, rushed in to arrest the male. Unbeknownst to him, the free-for-all had *really* excited the individual. So much so, he had masturbated and ejaculated in his hand while waiting for the cops to arrive.

When the officer came around the corner into the common area, a handful of semen was thrown in his face. When I say handful, this guy's oyster consumption must have been on point. If you don't know, oysters are high in zinc, and this mineral plays a critical role in sperm development. Measured against this incident, I must admit poop doesn't seem so bad after all. I'm guessing those booger particles from a sneeze aren't quite as offensive to you now either. But if you have a new-found fear of semen, otherwise known as spermophobia, I'm sorry for planting that seed.

As for my coworker who caught the now infamous money shot, he deserves some credit because he took it on the chin like a champ and even finished his shift. What's even more remarkable, he arrested the subject *who was still actively masturbating*. Yes . . . it was out, fully erect, and being primed again. Thank God the officer slapped the cuffs on him before a second round of fluids could be shared. On a happy note, none of the employees were seriously hurt, and the officer didn't suffer any long-term PTSD.

The crime? This one gets a little tricky. The main violations of law involved the multiple assaults on staff. The second crime committed was harassment. Throwing a glob of semen into someone's face without consent clearly constitutes offensive physical contact. But wait—we've got a trifecta of criminal activity. Since actively masturbating in front of a police officer is generally frowned upon, indecent exposure was tacked on as well. As a result, if you picked option 1, 2, or 3, congratulations—we'll consider the case cracked.

The Bad Bunny . . .

I was called out to a residence after our SWAT team had surrounded it. Inside of the house was an adult female who was armed with a handgun. She was home alone and had called a local hospital telling them she was going to kill people. My job was to talk her out peacefully. As you'll read later in this book, my specialty as a cop was as a hostage negotiator. This call fit into the no-big-deal category; we handled stuff like this routinely.

My fellow negotiator, Lenny Torres, responded to the call as well. Lenny possesses some serious skills and is considered one of our best. Let's put it this way: if I had a family member in crisis, I would want Lenny to talk to them.

Typically, for larger and more intense events, we bring out a negotiator bus. It has all the bells and whistles for any crisis situation. We wouldn't need it for this call, so we parked down the street in an unmarked police car. Time was on our side since we did not have anyone in immediate danger except for the female with the gun. I decided to be the primary negotiator and make a call inside the residence. Lenny would act in the capacity of a secondary negotiator, whose job is to remind me of anything I'm missing in the conversation. Two sets of ears are always better than one. In larger call outs, such as barricaded hostage situations, we will bring out an entire team. The team duties are as follows:

> **Primary Negotiator:** Deals directly with the subject to build rapport.
>
> **Secondary Negotiator:** Listens in, takes notes, and offers strategies.
>
> **Intel Negotiator:** Gathers information on subjects involved. We want to know everything about you, and that means *everything*: family members; lovers; work, medical, and criminal histories; pets; medications; hobbies; mental disorders; politics; sexual tendencies; military service; education; social media accounts; and more. If you prefer Coke over Pepsi, we want to know.
>
> **Team Leader:** Runs the show. The team leader is the liaison between command staff and negotiators to help avoid unnecessary distractions.

It's not uncommon for our first few attempts to contact the person in crisis to go unanswered. People in this situation usually don't want to talk to the cops. But negotiators can be much like teenage kids: we keep calling when we want something, we don't give up, and we blow up your phone until you answer. When the person does finally answer, we always start off by telling them our first name and who we are. It's usually not a secret as to why we are there, so honesty is the best policy. In my career, with hundreds of negotiations, this has held true 99.9 percent of the time.

Negotiations can last for hours or days, and recalling everything you said to an individual is nearly impossible. As we all know, remembering lies, in particular, is even more difficult. If a person catches you in a lie, you will quickly lose credibility and rapport. It's certainly not worth the risk. I teach new negotiators that lying in a negotiation is the kiss of death.

As for the 0.01 percent exception that I left out, this involves extraordinary circumstances where a homicidal maniac is on the verge of killing hostages. He needs to be brought close to a window for snipers. In this extremely rare instance, the truth will not work out very well, giving him more time to decide to kill hostages. The negotiators obviously can't be honest and ask, "Hey, do you mind coming to the window so we can kill you?" Instead, they say, "We are moving all the cops back like you wanted. Have a look for yourself." Again, it is an extreme case that requires extreme measures.

This is an unusual situation, but more typically, even with proven killers, we almost always choose to be honest. I have had murderers ask me if they are going to be arrested and taken to jail. Although I would soften my answer a little, I would have to tell the truth. I'd respond by saying, "You took a life today, and you have to answer for that." While this might seem counterintuitive, the suspect actually respects this honest answer. They already know what's going to happen, so if you lie or downplay it too much, it will come back to bite you. Bottom line: don't lie, because it usually causes communications to break down, often beyond repair. In a life-or-death situation, negotiators rarely have the luxury of a second chance.

Now, let's go back to the house with the female suspect armed with a handgun. You've got one chance, so . . . Name That Crime.

(Police photo)

1. **Distribution of Child Pornography.** According to Alaska Statute 11.61.125, "a person commits the crime of child pornography if the person distributes in this state or advertises, promotes, solicits, or offers to distribute in this state any material that is proscribed under AS 11.61.127 (related to possession of child pornography)."

2. **Terroristic Threatening.** According to Alaska Statute 11.56.810, "a person commits the crime of terroristic threatening in the second degree if the person makes a threat that a circumstance dangerous to human life or property exists or is about to exist with reckless disregard that the threat may place a person in reasonable fear of serious physical

injury to any person by means of a dangerous instrument and cause evacuation of or initiation of an emergency protocol for a building, public place or area, business premises, or mode of public transportation."

3. **Misconduct Involving Weapons in the Third Degree.**
According to Alaska Statute 11.61.200, "a person commits the crime of misconduct involving weapons in the third degree if the person knowingly possesses a firearm capable of being concealed on one's person after having been convicted of a felony or adjudicated a delinquent minor for conduct that would constitute a felony if committed by an adult by a court of this state, a court of the United States, or a court of another state or territory."

It was our lucky day: the female suspect answered the call on my first attempt. "Hi, this is Doug from the Anchorage Police Department." I followed up by asking her name, which she readily gave to me. A trace of the phone number and residence confirmed who it was; for the sake of anonymity, we'll just call her Bunny.

As negotiators, we do our best to ask open-ended questions that push the person in crisis to talk more. As a suspect, when you are talking—no matter the subject—you are providing valuable information. I asked Bunny what was going on that day to cause her to call the hospital. Again, this opening question can't be answered with a simple yes or no—by design. Many times, getting the conversation flowing is like pulling teeth. But, to my surprise, Bunny didn't hesitate to explain exactly what her intentions were. She calmly revealed that she had created a "death board" and intended to kill everyone on the list. The calmness in her voice, as well as her direct description of who was on the list, was particularly alarming. Since negotiators use emotions to our advantage, her calm deliberation threw me for a loop.

I asked Bunny to tell me more about the death board—who were the people on it and why? She went into a long explanation about how each one had wronged her in some way. She then told me she was from California and used to be a celebrity. Obviously, I was going to key in on this little tidbit. I asked, "Wow . . . were you an actress?" Bunny said she had done a few smaller films and some theater. Before I could tell her how cool that was, she said she was also a Playboy Playmate. In fact, she had been featured as the centerfold in this iconic magazine. The cherry on top: Hugh Hefner and she were good friends. I started to smile, not because I believed I had a Playboy Playmate on the line but just the opposite. I figured there wasn't a chance in hell. The odds of her being selected for the centerfold of *Playboy* would be about the same as me playing professional football for the Dallas Cowboys. But Bunny didn't stop there; she kept on going. Next, we heard all about her modeling career and photo shoots as well as a star-studded list of hunks she had dated.

I looked over at Lenny and had to hit the mute button as we both burst out laughing. Although this was a momentary lapse in professionalism, it couldn't be helped, but at least she never heard us. I told Lenny I had done a few major motion pictures myself, and he mentioned doing some modeling on the side.

With our thirty seconds of fun over, it was back to business. To be quite honest, all this time, Bunny had never stopped talking. I had to interrupt her, which is usually something negotiators don't do. I redirected her attention to the death board and asked how those people had wronged her. She talked about two attorneys she had hired to sue doctors. The doctors had apparently botched multiple plastic surgeries performed on her. Some of the doctors were in California, and some were in Alaska. The attorneys had since dropped her cases, and the doctors would no longer see her. Consequently, *she wanted them dead.*

I asked her if she had these names on an actual list? She said, "Oh, yes. I have it right in front of me, written down." My follow-up question was, "What other names are on the list?" Bunny went on to tell me about a couple of psychiatrists who didn't help her, a therapist who treated her poorly, and a tax accountant who screwed up her taxes. *She wanted them all dead.*

I mentioned to Bunny that, while people aren't always perfect, it doesn't mean they should die. As I continued about everyone deserving a second chance, she suddenly interrupted and asked, "Do you want me to finish telling you the list?" I was thinking to myself, *Mother of God, how long is it?* I then asked, "How many names are left?" Bunny excitedly answered, "Just one more." While I was guessing it might be an ex-husband, I played along and asked, "Okay, Bunny. Who is that person?" She matter-of-factly said, "It's my son." Startled, I repeated her answer back: "Did you say your son?" Without a crack in her voice: "Yes, my fifteen-year-old." *She wanted him dead.*

This is when things got a little more interesting. Bunny had amassed a total of nine names of people she unequivocally wanted to murder, including her teenage son. I immediately asked, "Why would you want to kill your son?" She gave an emotionless response, "I love him, but he has to die. The world is a bad place."

How could a mother say this? Maternal filicide is when a child is murdered by their own mother. In some cases, it involves psychosis, where the mother believes she is saving her child from a fate worse than death. Unfortunately, this occurs more often than one might think. For example, I worked a homicide scene where the mother killed all three of her kids and then calmly called 911 to report it. Her sole reason for the crime was to send them to a better place.

This triple homicide was particularly cruel when her premeditation is taken into consideration. She had mixed sleeping medication with Crystal Light, which was her kids' favorite drink. After they went to bed, she set her alarm to get up at 2:00 a.m. After she woke, she shot her oldest son in the head while he slept in his room. She left him there, set the alarm for several hours later, and went back to sleep. After the second alert, the next child was shot and killed. Once again, the mother went back to sleep after setting the alarm for a third time. But this time, she overslept, and when she awoke, the last child had already left for school. Unbelievably, the mother waited until early afternoon when the child returned home. The boy did not have a clue his two brothers lay executed in their bedrooms. As he played video games in the living room, the mother shot him in the back of the head.

Bunny's comment about killing her son had brought this tragic case back to mind. I cautiously asked her, "Where is your son now?" She said, "He's at school." Bunny let me know his name, what high school he went to, and that his normal routine was to take the bus home after school. A quick time check showed that his school was about to get out. Lenny touched base with the SWAT team to make sure the kiddo couldn't get into the house. A few officers were also tasked with watching out for him. We were assured everything was locked up tight; nobody was going in or coming out without our approval.

While on the phone, I could hear Bunny racking the slide of a handgun. Cops do this thousands of times in training, so I knew that sound very well. If you aren't familiar with how it works, racking allows for the ejection and loading of bullets. I asked Bunny, "What kind of gun do you have?" A long pause followed before she answered, "It's a Glock 45." I shared with her that I carried the same gun and asked how she liked it. Bunny said she loved it, telling me how easy it was to clean and how many bullets fit into the magazine. Since it's odd to be playing with a gun during a call with the cops, the possibility of suicide needed to be addressed.

"Bunny, are you going to hurt yourself with that gun?"

"Oh, no, I'm not."

"Bunny, are you going to hurt others with that gun?"

"Oh, yes, I am."

Throughout the entire conversation, Bunny was always polite, always direct, and showed absolutely no emotion when speaking of killing people. Her desire to take the life of her very own child was chilling to hear, even for seasoned negotiators. It was clear we would need to get Bunny some mental health treatment as soon as possible.

Over the next few minutes, we discussed some of these options. Bunny said she couldn't get help right now because she had to complete the list. Her son would be home soon, and she could start the plan. I told Bunny that police were surrounding her house, and I made it clear we could never let that happen. Her response surprised me: "What are you talking about?" It was at that moment when I realized that Bunny didn't know we were outside or, for that matter, that a SWAT team was present. When I had introduced myself as Doug from the police department, she had assumed it was only a courtesy call from headquarters to check on her.

This would turn out to be a good thing. Bunny quickly came to the realization that she couldn't go anywhere or kill anyone;

she'd have to give up. She even agreed to leave the Glock in a gun safe located in an upstairs bedroom. While I was waiting for her to put the gun away, Lenny and I did a celebratory fist bump. Whether she would have ultimately killed anyone or not, it's impossible to say, but negotiators love it when we save the day by convincing suspects to abort their plans.

As I was waiting on the phone with Bunny, another officer came running toward our car. Lenny jumped out to talk with him and then hurriedly got back in. Already knowing something was up, I muted the call.

We went from celebrating a win to maximum pucker factor in ten seconds. Why? Because the fifteen-year-old son had just walked into the house through the front door. Yes, it's true: SWAT had missed the kid coming home. *Holy fuck*, I thought to myself. *I better get a new game plan here—and fast!*

In the back of my mind, I was thinking that we were about to hear a gunshot. I was still on the phone with Bunny, so I asked her where she was at. Thank God—she was still trying to get the safe open in the upstairs bedroom. I told her to leave the gun somewhere in the room and to come outside. Bunny said it wasn't safe to leave guns out because accidents can happen. Incredibly, she did not have any idea her son was home. As SWAT was preparing to go in, I remembered our earlier conversation when Bunny was talking about her Glock. She said it was easy to clean, which meant she likely knew how to take it apart. I asked Bunny, "Do you know how to take your gun apart?" She confidently answered, "Of course. I take it apart all the time." This was my opening, and I was on pins and needles when I next asked, "Could you take it apart now for me? Because that would be the safe thing to do, and like you said, Bunny, accidents can happen."

The sweet sound of the slide being taken apart was music to my ears. With the gun inoperable, at least temporarily, SWAT went in. Bunny was taken into custody, and the son was found alive and well downstairs watching TV. The lessons were not over for this call, however—not by a long shot. It's usually a wrap for negotiators at this point, but SWAT wanted us to come inside and look at something.

First up was a lesson in humility. Negotiators can be know-it-alls, so this was a stark reminder that when somebody bares their soul, you should believe them until you know for certain otherwise. In Bunny's bedroom were multiple copies of a *Playboy* magazine with the centerfolds open. It was 100 percent Bunny in the flesh. The centerfold was also professionally framed above her bed. Additional photographs demonstrated that she was indeed a Hollywood personality and had dated some stars. While this was many years back, everything Bunny had said to me was true.

The death board was the real deal as well. It was a large paper pad displayed on an easel. Each name was written out with the word "kill" next to it. Going back through the over-sized pages—the type you flip over one by one—revealed additional information related to Bunny's deranged mental state. She had material that suggested she experienced erotophono-philia—and "sick" doesn't even begin to describe this perversion. This term is sometimes referred to as "lust murder," which is the sexual arousal or gratification when you fantasize about murder or actually kill someone. It doesn't mean you have sex with the body; rather, the homicidal act is enough to get you off. She also had drawings representing some of this crude behavior, images I won't soon forget. Between a death board, killing your own kid, and erotophonophilia, Bunny had some serious demons inside of her head.

As far as criminal charges for the Playboy Playmate, if you picked terroristic threatening . . . thumbs up! Besides the imminent threat to her teenage son, she also threatened the hospital and staff. When all was said and done, Bunny would receive a one-way ticket to a psychiatric hospital.

CHAPTER TWO

WHY SHARING ISN'T ALWAYS CARING

It's hard to ease into a book like this, so hopefully Name That Crime did its job and warmed you up a little in preparation for what is to come. Our parents taught us many things, including to never be selfish and to always share with others. They repeated this mantra to us with a wonderful sense of genuineness, reminding us often that it is better to give than to receive. In fairness, our folks meant well and couldn't have imagined why sharing isn't always caring. But the following examples of human indecency will prove that being selfish is sometimes the right thing to do.

Come Again . . .

In my previous story of the "Germaphobe's Worst Nightmare," the surprise money shot to the cop's face was as distasteful as it gets. But before we leave the land of semen throwing, let's consider the frequency of this activity. This behavior can't possibly be a thing now . . . or can it? I hate to be the bearer of

29

bad news, but this disgusting act is trending up. It has become so prevalent that in Portland, Oregon, the police bureau was forced to put out a public announcement warning about none other than a semen-tossing spree. Eventually, they would catch a forty-eight-year-old man named Manuel Banuelos-Alcala, linking him to four separate cases of throwing or smearing semen on women in area grocery stores. The justice system *really* threw the book at him—Manuel received a staggering sentence of *probation* for traumatizing people with his ejaculate. Somehow the courts, in this case, missed the part about the punishment fitting the crime.

In Alabama, apparently the greeting card section in Target can be ground zero for semen flinging. An unsuspecting woman was shopping for a Mother's Day card when she was hit with an unknown substance. In her court testimony, the victim said, "I felt a liquid on the right side of my face and felt it dripping down." Not having any idea what had happened, she used the restroom to wash it off. She then left the store and had lunch at a nearby restaurant. When she came out to her car, she noticed a yellow sticky note on her windshield, written by her assailant. It was three shocking words: "It was semen."

This sick son of a bitch had followed her. He wanted her to know exactly what he had done; it was all part of the thrill. Luckily for the cops, some of the excess liquid had stained the victim's shirt, and she was smart enough not to have washed it off. Store surveillance would show the suspect stalking the woman while she shopped and then following her into the parking lot. However, despite having the video, police could not identify the male and were at a standstill in the investigation. But the strange addiction of casting cum onto others would lead our suspect back to that very same greeting card section eight days later. This time, a very observant loss prevention officer recognized the male and called police. The cops were able to arrest him as he attempted to get away. The suspect, twenty-eight-year-old Deanuntea Caldwell, denied sharing his fluids but did admit to leaving the note on the victim's car. A subsequent DNA analysis showed Caldwell was, in fact, the sperm donor.

Would the justice system get it right this time? Not even close. Alabama did not have a law prohibiting such behavior. City prosecutor Brad Ekdahl would say, "Unfortunately, there is no law in Alabama that says you can't throw semen on someone." Considering that, what did the perpetrator get? He was sentenced to ninety days in jail for misdemeanor harassment. Due to the explosion of similar cases throughout the nation, states are scrambling to establish laws to combat this shameful perversion. Alabama quickly enacted a state law preventing any assaults with bodily fluids. They list the fluids as blood, saliva, seminal fluid, mucus, urine, or feces. If you are wondering why Deanuntea Caldwell always picked the greeting card section to send his boys flying, he was probably motivated purely by sentiment. After all, Hallmark's slogan is "When you care enough to send the very best."

If you think that skipping Target and going to Walmart instead might be a solution for avoiding the sharing of such fluids, well, I've got news for you: it really doesn't matter where you go. According to police reports, the following account would ruin anyone's Wally World shopping experience. A twenty-two-year-old Delaware man named Frank J. Short Jr. tossed a glob of his own semen onto the buttocks, thigh, and leg of a female he considered "hot." After doing so, he was nice enough to say to her, "Excuse me." As if it that wasn't creepy enough, with his eye now on the prize, Short continued to follow the woman around the store, intently staring at his accomplishment. The victim was forced to run into a back office and seek help from employees.

Police were called, and they arrested Short. Unbelievably, he was still hanging out at the store waiting for her when they arrived. When it comes to making first impressions, sometimes being bold is good, but Frank may have crossed that fine line of coming on a little too strong. When confronted by cops, he initially tried to downplay the incident, but he would later admit to being a "loner" who "gets a thrill out of such an act."[3] Police suspected him of doing this for many years prior to being caught. Short was finally convicted of offensive touching of another with saliva, urine, feces, or other bodily fluid (in this case, semen). He was also found guilty of lewdness. Surely, he got some serious time in the slammer, right? Unfortunately, like the other incidents, Short escaped any real penalty and received a pitiful six months' probation on each count with additional time suspended. We should all be a little salty with the courts' lack of just punishment in these cases.

Hold the Anchovies . . .

While the unwanted sharing of personal liquids is nasty, we're about to ratchet up the intensity, because Alaska has its own special flavor of taboo. As a matter of fact, one of the events in this chapter is considered the *grand champion* of sickening police stories. This accolade has been proven scientifically through random trials, in which cops across our nation, upon hearing the story,

[3] Ryan Gorman, *Pervert Admits to Throwing His Semen on 'Hot' Female Shopper at Delaware Wal-Mart*, (Daily Mail, 2013). https://www.dailymail.co.uk/news/article-2361534/Pervert-admits-throwing-semen-hot-female-shopper-Delaware-Wal-Mart.html. Article also available at: dougfifer.com.

expressed abject, universal disgust. (Okay, "scientifically proven" is a stretch, but you get the idea.)

First off, an important reminder about human biology: the pharyngeal reflex, better known as gagging, is the body's fail-safe mechanism to prevent us from choking or swallowing harmful substances. There are two basic causes for gagging: either a sensory stimulus or a mental image. The sensory trigger can include a smell, sound, sight, taste, or touch. It can be as simple as brushing your teeth, eating spoiled food, or participating in the act of oral sex. We have all experienced this, but activating that gag reflex with only mental imagery requires next-level disgust. The severity of that revulsion must be off the charts for battle-scarred cops to dry heave. As we continue with this next story, it might not be a bad idea to grab a barf bag before we soar into nauseating new heights.

America's favorite comfort food is undeniably pizza. A recent Harris poll showed an overwhelming majority choosing this as their favorite.[4] Pizza was twice as popular as the closest contenders of chocolate and ice cream. Finishing out the list, in order, were mac and cheese, chips, hamburgers, steak, popcorn, pasta, and Mexican food. Sixty-seven percent, or two-thirds of all Americans, say they turn to these yummy delights as a mood booster. Globally, pizza is by far the most Instagrammed food on planet Earth. A mind-blowing thirty-seven million posts and hashtags pay tribute to this Italian cuisine, which originated as far back as 600 BC. What do we crave on our pizza? The traditional toppings of pepperoni, mushrooms, and sausage are among our favorites.

---

[4] Amy Reiter, *Guess What America's Favorite Comfort Food Is*, (FN Dish, 2016). https://www.foodnetwork.com/fn-dish/news/2016/02/guess-what-americas-favorite-comfort-food-is. Article also available at: dougfifer.com.

The most disliked addition is the unloved anchovy. These small green and blue fish are salted in brine, cured, and pack a powerful punch when added as a topping.

According to *The Washington Post*, we eat one hundred acres of pizza daily—that's three billion pizzas annually, which works out to a yearly total of forty-six slices, or twenty-three pounds, for every person in the country. It's estimated around 17 percent of all restaurants in the U.S. are pizzerias. We have undeniably established pizza as the king of comfort food. With these jaw-dropping consumption numbers, it seems inevitable that law enforcement and pizza would share a few stories together. In my career, I've been involved in investigating several robberies where the suspect ordered to a location, only to rip off the unsuspecting delivery driver. On one occasion, the perpetrator even took the pizza and forgot to demand the cash. I think it's safe to say that committing a felony to get a pizza takes the term "hangry" to a new level. Another time, a delivery driver contacted me about suspected drug trafficking at a house. The residents had offered the driver drugs in exchange for the pizza, and when the driver declined, they unwisely threw a small bag of pills at him and slammed the door shut. And yes, when he reported the incident, he still had the pills, which turned out to be OxyContin. Although this might represent the bartering system at its finest, we subsequently traded the dopers' freedom for a jail cell.

Nationally, pizza and crime intersect in some outlandish ways. You might recall the famous pizza bomber case involving Brian Douglas Wells, who died in 2003 as a result of a detonated explosive device. Brian had been delivering pizza to a remote location in Erie, Pennsylvania. The suspects at this location held him at gunpoint, fastened a real bomb around his neck, and gave him nine pages of elaborate instructions to rob a bank. In addition, he was provided with a homemade shotgun resembling a cane. Wells was told that any contact with the authorities would result in the detonation of the bomb. He followed their directions and provided a bank teller with a note demanding $250,000. After getting only $8,702, he attempted his getaway.

A witness inside the bank called police, who arrested Wells a short time later. He quickly told them about the bomb and that he'd be killed unless his instructions were followed to completion. Police cleared the area, moved back from Wells, and called the bomb squad. Unfortunately, the device detonated a short time later, blowing a large hole in Wells' chest. He was killed almost instantly while the dramatic event unfolded live on television. Three of the convicted suspects have since died in prison; a fourth suspect was given immunity for his testimony. According to law enforcement reports, Wells had been, in fact, a likely participant in the original planning of the bank robbery. Unbeknownst to him, a double-cross was put into play as his coconspirators had changed the plan in order to eliminate him as a witness. This perplexing and unorthodox crime has garnered mass media attention fueled by public interest. In 2018, Netflix released a series about the incident called *Evil Genius: The True Story of America's Most Diabolical Bank Heist*.

Can pizza crust itself catch a serial killer? When we think of crust, the normal debate usually revolves around it needing to be thin or thick. Beyond that, we wouldn't think of it as being that important. Lonnie Franklin Jr., however, was sentenced to die thanks to the crust of some leftover pizza pie. Convicted of killing ten women and suspected of murdering twenty-five more, he was sentenced to death in 2016. The FBI defines the term "serial killing" as "a series of three or more killings, not less than one of which was committed within the United States, having common characteristics such as to suggest the reasonable possibility that the crimes were committed by the same actor or actors."[5] Detectives caught a break in this serial killer case when Franklin's son, Christopher, was arrested on weapons charges. Under California law, adults arrested for any felony offense are subject to DNA collection. This has been legally challenged but affirmed as constitutional by the courts. After taking a cheek swab from Christopher, detectives used a familial DNA search to identify his father as the suspected killer.

A traditional DNA search checks to see if a particular person matches a profile. Familial DNA expands this to include any relatives, thereby potentially linking family members to unsolved crimes. Law enforcement is quickly expanding the use of DNA matching using investigative genetic genealogy. DNA obtained at a crime scene can lawfully be compared to all genetic genealogy databases. Companies such as Ancestry, FamilySearch, or 23andMe must comply with search warrants. Ancestry's own privacy statement, listed on their website, says it does not voluntarily cooperate with law enforcement. The company does acknowledge they require a valid legal process, identified as a court order or search warrant, prior to complying with any requests. All the large genealogy companies offer similar disclosures. Despite their objections, DNA, or deoxyribonucleic acid, is a game changer for investigators. It is contained in virtually every human substance: blood, skin, bone, teeth, hair, semen, perspiration, fingernails, urine, vomit, and feces, to mention just a few.

---

[5] Robert J. Morton, *Serial Murder: Multi-Disciplinary Perspectives for Investigators*, (U.S. Department of Justice, Federal Bureau of Investigation, 2023). https://www.fbi.gov/stats-services/publications/serial-murder. Article also available at: dougfifer.com.

If you ever watch *CSI*, it is impressive how quickly they solve crimes based on a minute piece of evidence left at the scene. I can tell you from personal experience that it is certainly not as effortless or glamorous as the show depicts. The Anchorage Police Department has a crime scene team that investigates all homicides and suspicious deaths. I worked in this unit for many years and forensically mapped countless murders. Investigators like me analyze and process evidence using Locard's exchange principle, which holds that a perpetrator will always bring something to a crime scene and leave with something from it. Dr. Edmond Locard is considered one of the foremost experts on forensic science techniques and was regarded as the "Sherlock Holmes" of France. He died in 1966, but his words still ring true today: "It is impossible for a criminal to act, especially considering the intensity of a crime, without leaving traces of this presence."[6]

In the case of Lonnie Franklin Jr., he left multiple traces of semen and saliva on his victims. Although authorities had previously linked his genetic profile through a familial DNA search, it would not be enough to warrant a guilty verdict. They would somehow need to collect and match his present-day DNA. Considered one of the most prolific murderers in history, Franklin roamed free during his killing spree for an estimated twenty-five years until his luck finally ran out. While attending a birthday party at a restaurant called John's Incredible Pizza, he unwittingly left some pizza crust on his plate. It was collected by an undercover detective posing as a busboy. Fortunately, it contained enough DNA to positively connect Franklin. Some might say

---

[6] *Edmond Locard,* (Crime Museum, 2023). https://www.crimemuseum.org/crime-library/forensic-investigation/edmond-locard/. Article also available at: dougfifer.com.

naming your pizza joint "incredible" is a little pretentious, but after this case, there's no doubt that "in crust we trust." Lonnie Franklin Jr., awaiting execution on death row, died in his prison cell of natural causes in 2020.

I would be remiss if I didn't include a strip club connection to pizza. The following events took place in Albuquerque, New Mexico, at a naughty nightclub called The Ice House. Local cops had been called to this establishment numerous times for a variety of crimes. This night's complaint was promptly referred to the health department, because—well, let's just say the officers did not want any part of this show. Dancer Stephanie Evans was being promoted as "The Human Super Soaker." Dubbed as a must-see attraction, she was able to shoot Ping-Pong balls and water over twenty-five feet from her vagina onto patrons, a dubiously hygienic act which led to the original police call. The local health department conducted a follow-up investigation by sending an undercover agent to see if there were any health code violations. The agent watched the show and verified that the audience was indeed getting super soaked. But that wasn't the main issue with the health department—nope, it was that pizza was being served during the act.

The findings established the outgoing vaginal liquid was contaminating the pizza, which posed a health threat. The city representative—and you can't make this up—also sampled a slice. He reported the temperature was around eighty degrees. The city's food and beverage ordinance requires that pizza be maintained at 140 degrees while not being eaten. As if a rogue wave from a woman's nether regions gushing onto the pizza wasn't enough, this public servant went the extra mile to document the lack of proper temperature by eating the pizza. His report also related that approximately fifteen Ping-Pong balls had been inserted, yes, *there*, and ejected into the crowd. Many onlookers caught the balls with their hands, but one "lucky" bastard, presumably with tongue in cheek, snatched it with his mouth.

In the end, the city of Albuquerque's legal department hand-delivered a notice of compliance to the owner of the club. The first violation stated, "As required by the Food and Beverage Ordinance, all pizza not being eaten must be stored in a hot holding device which will maintain an internal temperature of 140 degrees Fahrenheit." Well, I'll be damned, they certainly blew the whistle on that one. The second and presumably *lesser* violation stated, "No food or drink whatsoever can be served during any performance that involves expelling fluids or other objects from a vagina."

As outlandish as these stories seem to be, none of them will likely diminish your love for pizza. The mere thought of stopping yourself from scarfing down those forty-six slices, equaling twenty-three pounds of America's number one comfort food, is a nonstarter. And I would probably agree with you—if I hadn't been involved in the following events that curtailed my pizza cravings for life.

Being a street cop is an adrenaline junkie's dream job. You can go from zero to a hundred at any moment. I worked patrol for many years and lived for that rush of excitement. Officers are assigned to specific areas, which enable a faster response, as things often happen quickly and unexpectedly. I've always related the famous *Forrest Gump* movie quote to police work: "Life is like a box of chocolates. You never know what you're gonna get." I like this metaphor because chocolates come in all shapes, sizes, and flavors. What comes next over the police airwaves can be straightforward, challenging, or death defying—quite literally, you never know what you're gonna get.

For those of you who want to sample a little cop chocolate, there are a few options. Police ride-along programs are designed to give the average citizen a firsthand view of what being a cop is like. Most people have very little insight into what occurs criminally in their respective communities. It is a unique experience for those seeking to learn more about what law enforcement does on a regular basis. It's all too common nowadays to get bombarded with misinformation about police officers. Ride-alongs can help change that perception by allowing the career to be viewed in its rawest form. You get to witness the decisions cops make, often in a split second, as well as the challenges they encounter.

I've taken friends, family, and community members on ride-alongs throughout my career. Without exception, they are amazed at how busy and difficult the job can be. What's more, they can't believe what goes on in their neck of the woods. It's an enlightening experience, and I highly recommend you consider participating in this program if it's available in your area. Most local PDs offer this opportunity, so strap on that vest and put humanity to the test. For those of you who may never get the chance, let's do a reading "ride-along" right now. It's time for you to play cop, so let's see if you've got what it takes.

It's "go" time—you've donned your uniform, and you're looking sharp. Oh yeah—I forgot to mention those thirty pounds of gear. First-timers always feel that weight. The bulletproof vest, gun, baton, handcuffs, taser, pepper spray, and flashlight can seem like a ton of bricks. My advice? Just suck it up, rookie—we've got work to do. Dispatch has given us the call sign of 45C—pay attention and try not to forget it. Forty-five is the area we'll be patrolling, and the C stands for "Charlie" shift. A ten-hour marathon from 3:00 p.m. to 1:00 a.m. starts now. We're in a marked police unit, coffee in hand. Let's see what flavor of chocolate the next call brings.

> DISPATCH: 45C, stand by to copy . . .
>
> YOU: (*Completely oblivious to the chatter as you look at all the cool equipment in the cop car. There's a shotgun, rifle, video camera, computer, radar, and unfamiliar switches everywhere. You feel like a kid in a candy store.*)
>
> DISPATCH: 45C, 45 Charlie, 45, do you copy? (*Each time with a little more insistence.*)
>
> OFFICER FIFER: Relax, every rookie misses their call sign. That's why I told you to listen up and not forget. (*Pause.*) Well . . . are you going to answer now?
>
> YOU: (*Picking up the radio mic.*) 45C, I'm ready to copy.
>
> DISPATCH: 45C, respond to the area of Hillside and De Armoun Road for a suspicious vehicle in the neighborhood.
>
> YOU: 45C copies and en route.
>
> OFFICER FIFER: Nice job, rook.

We get a whole lot more information sent to us via computer. An exact address of the complainant, vehicle description, and most importantly, why the caller thinks it's suspicious. In this case, a neighbor was concerned due to a truck being parked at a dead end. The vehicle was running and had fogged up windows and a pizza delivery sign attached to the roof. The complainant did not know if the truck was occupied or how long it had been parked there.

Cops are usually given the caller's contact number. This way, if something seems out of the ordinary or we have additional questions, we can call ourselves. A suspicious vehicle is about as common as cop work gets. It was also wintertime in Alaska, which means it's cold and not atypical for windows to fog. Another common cause is when the occupants are having sex. The pizza delivery sign most likely negates the latter, so the driver is probably just parked there for a minute. We've all stopped to make a phone call, take a leak, or merely to rest, and that's likely what the driver is doing.

You might think we should call the complainant and find out what pizza company is on the delivery sign. That way, we could check with the business to see if a driver was delivering in the area. Nice thought, Columbo, but it's a busy night and calls are stacking up. We've got enough information, so let the games begin. By the way, the beat we are working is an affluent area, one of the wealthiest in Anchorage. It's only about 4:00 p.m., but it's already getting dark. Welcome to the trials and tribulations of living up north; darkness comes quickly during the winter months. It's also snowing heavily, which will slow our roll a bit. On the bright side, this might be to our advantage, as, hopefully, the truck has moved on prior to our arrival.

No such luck, partner: look what we rolled up on. It's exactly as described, a pizza delivery truck parked at the dead end of a neighborhood. And sure enough, the windows are still fogged up. Now, for legal and confidentiality reasons, we're not going to name the pizza company here. I will share that it's in the top three national chains. Our patrol lights and headlights are off because we prefer a stealthy method of approach. Since the vehicle is facing away, we can't tell if anyone is inside. We wait in our vehicle for a few minutes, watching. You want to jump out and rain terror down, but I remind you that a game plan might be helpful. It's a two-seater truck and the rear window is completely steamed up. Together, we deduce two likely scenarios. First, the driver is smoking some serious weed. If you didn't know, marijuana has been legal in Alaska since 1975 after Ravin v. State. The second possibility: the pizzamobile has turned into a shaggin' wagon. Whatever the case, it seems our occupant(s) are unaware of our presence.

It's up to you, rookie. What should we do?

(a) Kick on the overhead lights, flash those blue and reds, and maybe tap the siren?

(b) Since it's not illegal to park in the area, maybe we leave?

(c) Get out and see what's going on?

I'm going to give you a gold star if we get out and see what's going on. We're the cops, and we can't simply leave when called because we have concerned neighbors. We don't kick on the overheads because we'll lose the element of surprise. If the occupant has a gun, we want to be the first to engage. How are we going to approach the vehicle? You want me to take the driver's side and you take the passenger's side? Solid choice—this might be your true calling.

As we start to close in, I can see the excitement in your eyes. It's your first ride-along, your maiden voyage as a fellow crime fighter, and you're about to get your cherry popped. I'm fairly certain at this point that we've got nothing more than two people fucking. I didn't tell you, but that much steaminess can't be weed alone. You're about to experience some rather unsettling, nasty fornication, because in police work, good naked is a rare find.

We're now at the back of the truck, inching up on either side. We have our flashlights in hand. Guns remain secure in our holsters since we don't have an immediate threat. We move in unison and reach the driver and passenger side windows. The occupants cannot see us because we are shielded by part of the vehicle frame, commonly called B-pillars, which are located behind the front doors. Cops use these as protection because metal is always safer than glass. We ease in, just enough to see. The side windows are still partially fogged, and it takes a bit for our eyes to adjust. Slowly, an image emerges of a male in the driver's seat. I can't quite see the passenger seat, so I motion to you and mouth, "Anybody there?" You whisper back, "It's empty except for a pizza carrier."

I quickly refocus on the male, who is completely oblivious to our presence. It's still hard to make out what he's doing . . . wait a minute—oh, no! I knew there was sex involved; I just didn't predict he would be stroking his salami. It is almost as if the universe slows a bit as I see him playing tug of war with his member, over and over again. I immediately motion for you to look in because it's true—misery loves company. I see the astonishment on your face; this isn't what you signed up for. Now, as if this couldn't get any weirder, I notice an interesting thing about his penis. It isn't erect, but he is nonetheless pulling it for all it's worth—again and again, like an overcooked spaghetti noodle. I look at you, then the noodle, then back to you, then the noodle, back and forth, for what feels like an eternity. Finally, I snap myself back to reality. I briefly wonder why we're both so engrossed with a guy choking his limp chicken. In my defense, could you avoid staring?

Okay, partner, what should we do?

(a) We still don't have a crime; let's walk away.

(b) "Knock knock, who's there?"

(c) Yell, "What the fuck are you doing?"

When in doubt, yelling "What the fuck are you doing" usually works. I'll give you a newbie pass on this one and do the honors myself. I am a human bullhorn, and the message is sent with vigor. To my surprise, he doesn't freeze; instead, he immediately jumps out of the vehicle with no time to put it away, no time to pull up his pants—just time to jump out and stand there in bewilderment. Instinctively, I step back several feet, keeping two things in mind. This guy might be high on dope, but more importantly, he has his dick out. Before anything else, I ask if he could please pull up his pants. Luckily, he complies and covers it up. Oddly, he keeps muttering something softly under his breath. Eventually, he says it loud enough to be heard: "I've done something bad." I think to myself, *Well, jacking off in your delivery vehicle* is *kind of bad.*

He won't stop saying it: "I've done something bad. I've done something bad." He is also profusely sweating in near-freezing temperatures. A thorough pat-down of his person and check of the truck do not uncover any weapons. My mind quickly goes to a previous case where the suspect used the exact same wording. It ended up as a domestic-related homicide, where the husband had brutally stabbed his wife to death. He then called into dispatch and demanded to talk with an officer. They forwarded his call to my cell phone. His first words to me: "I've done something bad." Using GPS, we later located him dragging his murdered wife into the Alaskan woods on a sled. Could my pizza delivery driver be a killer? Cops from time to time get a Spidey sense, a feeling something terrible has happened. I am certainly sensing something is off here, but even I can't imagine how far off I will be from the truth.

When asked, he readily gives his name as Stan. Our goal is to establish a rapport with suspects, no matter how repulsive their crimes might be. Even though he was playing with his dick minutes earlier, I tell him it isn't a big deal and not to worry about it. It is possible he was simply overwhelmed by the police contact while doing the naughty by himself. It's also possible he just committed a burglary, rape, or murder. Interrogations are like a chess match; each question and subsequent question becomes more important to get right. If they're too weak, you won't get traction; if they're too strong, the suspect will shut down. You're up to bat again, rookie, so what's our best strategy?

(a) Ask what he was doing in the neighborhood.

(b) Take him back to the station for a formal interview.

(c) Ask him why he is so upset.

We ask him why he's so upset because wanting to know why someone is upset signifies that we care about their well-being and want to help. This holds true even if the suspect has killed someone: we still want to help—help put that person in prison forever. In this case, our guy is more than willing to talk. He appreciates us asking why he is upset, and so his account of that remarkable day begins.

Stan is a tall and lanky white male, early thirties, balding, and not particularly handsome. He has smoker's teeth, a pock-marked face, and is generally disheveled looking. He says he is going to get fired from his job and probably go to jail for what he has done. I ask Stan if he is upset at us for catching him masturbating. To put him at ease, I tell him we all do it, but perhaps we can choose better places. He says that isn't it—what he had done is "really bad." I am internally screaming, "Spit it out!" but externally, I keep my composure. I think to myself, *Holy shit, I'm about to solve a homicide*, because "really bad" in police work typically signifies death, and the opportunity to take a murderer off the streets is about as good as it gets.

I ask Stan to tell me what happened because we want to help him. He mentions delivering pizza to a nearby residence, so I follow up with, "What happened at that residence? Did somebody get hurt?" He quickly denies it: "I didn't hurt anyone. I just delivered a pizza." His hands are trembling, and I can see the sweat pouring off his forehead—some serious red flags in police work. I tell him it will be hard for me to help if I don't know what happened, and I'll have to detain him and check all the nearby houses to make certain everyone is okay. Stan then makes a rather alarming statement: "I like her a lot, but it's too late now." Okay, 100 percent—this guy's a killer.

Well, rook, we are stepping up your stress level here a bit. What's our next play?

(a) "What's the address you delivered to?"

(b) Repeat his statement back to him as a question: "Stan, you said you like her, but it's too late now?"

(c) Put this criminal in handcuffs; he deserves the electric chair.

We are going with option (b) because it's our best chance to keep him talking. We continually use his name as a show of respect, and we repeat what he says to convey that we are listening while asking open-ended questions to keep him talking. Cops are savvy in knowing when someone wants to let their demons out, and these tactics are very effective. It works like a charm; he starts off, "It's a lady I always deliver pizza to up the street. I don't know her name, but I like her a lot. She isn't hurt, but I did something to the pizza."

I'm not quite picking up what he's putting down. I think maybe this guy poisoned the pizza, so I ask, "What did you do to the pizza, Stan?" He shakes his head, and his lips start quivering, but he can't say it. I gently prod him. "I need to know everyone is safe."

It is the shot heard round the world when Stan blurts out, "I masturbated on the pizza." I'm as stunned as you are, rookie. This is a first for both of us! As odd as it may sound, I'm not exactly sure what he means. I get what jerking off is, but the details are what's important. Suffice it to say, masturbation can have many different outcomes. Did he just roll his dick around the pizza? Or was he more aggressive by taking the crust to pound town? What, oh, what, did Stan the Man do? You know it gets worse, but rather than being appalled, you're feeling a little excitement. It's okay. Welcome to the club; this is what cops live for. I'm happy we're sharing this moment together because it's not every day a guy blows his load all over a steaming hot pizza pie.

For most people, this one encounter would be enough to strip off your uniform, turn in that badge, and never look back again. But not you, partner. You're in it to win it. You can't deny it—the only thing on your mind right now is cum pizza. If I'm wrong, feel free to stop the reading ride-along and seek out a safe space. If I'm right—and I'm confident I am—let's finish popping your police cherry, shall we?

Why would criminals ever want to openly and freely tell the cops of their wrongdoings? It's called "catharsis psychology," based on the release of pent-up emotions. The term "catharsis" originates from the Greek word *katharsis*, meaning "purification" or "cleansing." Keeping emotions bottled up feels bad, so it's a natural relief to let them out. Think about when you've told a lie and the stress that followed. Now, think about when you've corrected a lie and the immediate relief you felt. Catharsis spans the gamut, no matter the indiscretion, from a little white lie to a gruesome murder. Emotional pain can be the ultimate truth serum.

Stan desperately wanted to spill his guts and, boy, did he ever self-disclose. You're probably thinking you might have this one figured out. Let's see how spot on you are. Choose one of the following reasons for his behavior.

(a) As a show of dominance over women, Stan does this to every pizza he delivers.

(b) He is having an affair with the resident, a housewife, and this is foreplay.

(c) He has a secret crush on the resident and sexually fantasizes about her.

Option (c) is correct, but let's add a bit of context. Stan did indeed have some rather salacious feelings for the unsuspecting pizza connoisseur. He was so infatuated, he'd regularly ejaculate onto her pizza prior to delivery. Now, being the gentleman he is, Stan took the time to rub the seminal fluid around the pie. This served two purposes. First of all, he wanted to make sure every bite was marked with his manhood. And second of all, Stan did not want to get caught by leaving a puddle of splooge. At this moment, we thought someone was going to run up to us with a TV camera and say, "Smile, you're on *Candid Camera*." But no such luck here—this was the real deal.

Think back to how we found Stan when he was in a tug of war with flaccidity. Well, Stan isn't quite done with his purification and cleansing. He admits to trying to masturbate at the thought of the woman eating his cum. The only problem is that he had recently deposited his load and couldn't get it up for the second go-around. Even as a seasoned cop, I was still dumbstruck. I had no clue what to do—a rarity in my career.

You pick what's next:

(a) Tell Stan about the benefits of Viagra and Cialis?

(b) Call the DA (district attorney)?

(c) Contact the female and recover any uneaten pizza?

This time, it's both (b) and (c). We'll start by calling the Anchorage district attorney's office. Cops are given two small law books, called "field manuals," for state and munici-pal statutes. We use these to look up crimes when they get a little tricky. In this case, however, the crime for adding sperm to take-out food wasn't really covered in the manual. I remem-ber that call to the on-duty prosecutor like it was yesterday. The pause on the other end after explaining the graphic details was painfully long. Then came the clarification ques-tion back to me: "Did you say he ejaculated on a pizza?"

"Yes," I replied, "that is correct."

"Did the woman eat the pizza?"

"We haven't contacted her yet."

"Go and get the pizza or any uneaten portion ASAP. I'll also need a few minutes to research a chargeable offense, so call me back."

The DA was as stumped as I was. Now I moved forward with option (c), contacting the resident and recovering the evidence. Guess what? There was no longer any evidence to recover. Yup, it was a personal size and had been completely devoured. Needless to say, it was rather uncomfortable telling her that the secret was quite literally in the sauce. I told her the truth, the whole truth, and nothing but the truth. Let's fast-forward through the emotional carnage that followed, though; I'll just let you imagine being in her shoes.

I called the prosecutor back in anticipation of taking this sick bastard to jail, but the DA still didn't have an answer and seemed even more perplexed this time around. He was highly concerned about the lack of evidence (i.e., the lack of pizza), even though we had an admission. He asked, "Does the suspect have any communicable diseases?" I thought to myself, *How in the hell would I know?* Hey, partner, can *you* go ask Chef Boyardee if he's got gonorrhea, HIV, HPV, pubic lice, syphilis, herpes, hepatitis, or chlamydia? Be honest with me—you must be loving cop work by now. What other job can combine a question about STDs with cum pizza? What's that, rook? He said he was clean? Sounds good. I'll let the DA know our pizza molester promised he was free of any crotch crickets.

This is when things got even more interesting. The prosecutor said, "I don't think we have a viable charge here." Now, that long awkward pause had been reversed, and I had a clarifying question: "Did you say we don't have a criminal charge?" You'll never guess—Alaska did not have a criminal statute preventing such an act.

Where do we go from here, my fellow crime fighter?

(a) Take Stan for a ride up to Yellowstone's infamous train station?

(b) Let Stan go, write a report, and see what's next in the call load?

(c) Grab some Xanax for our newfound anxiety disorder?

The words, "You are free to go, Stan," still echo in my mind to this day. Option (b), by law, was all we had. Yes, we contacted his employer, who immediately relieved Stan of employment. If there was a silver lining, it was that the Anchorage Police Department would be making national news very soon. I even took the time to mentally prepare some thoughts should a reporter come calling. My fellow cops started a betting pool as to how much the civil settlement would be. Look at that, my fellow Five-O. Your first call is going to result in us getting our fifteen minutes of fame. News flash: fame never came. I'd forgotten about the power of money and that the almighty dollar would prevail. Big business quickly came calling, a nondisclosure agreement was signed by the victim, and the rest is history. It's unlikely we'll ever know what that settlement number was, but it was rumored to be in the seven figures. This brings up one hell of a personal question: would you hold the anchovies if a million dollars was on the line? Oh, and by the way, Alaska now has a criminal statute that prohibits pumping and dumping on a pizza pie.

Stings Like a Bee . . .

So far, you've learned that semen-flinging is trending up and cum pizza is but a fast-food delivery away, which begs the question:

what else could possibly be left? It should come as no surprise that sexual deviants will continue to astonish us with their perverted ingenuity. Living proof is a man named Thomas Byron Stemen. In 2020, he stabbed a woman with a syringe in a Maryland supermarket. After injecting her in her buttocks, he told the victim, "I know, it feels like a bee sting, doesn't it?" Cops would eventually track this backstabber down using video surveillance captured at the store. Stemen was arrested with a loaded syringe on him and several more in his car. A later search of his home would find even more. They were sent to the crime lab for testing, and all were found to contain Stemen's semen. He was sentenced to ten years in prison and is believed to have many more unreported victims. Although Stemen never admitted his reasoning for the disgusting attack, I've got a sneaking suspicion he shared the same fantasy as pizza boy.[7]

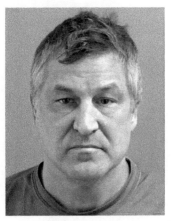

(Booking photo)

---

[7] Check out the crime in action (after all, seeing is believing): https://youtu.be/4dAsOy-QNMk. Video also viewable at: dougfifer.com.

CHAPTER THREE

KINK AND INK

"Think before you ink" is level-headed advice, but reality will soon show that it's far more apropos than you might know. It's estimated around 30 percent to 35 percent of Americans have tattoos, and of those, one in four regrets getting their permanent ink. Despite this buyer's remorse, getting tatted seems to be on the rise. Gen Z and Millennials are driving this renewed popularity using social media. And flexin' their ink on Instagram, with more than 1.6 billion users worldwide, seems to be working. The industry has grown an average of 8.4 percent between 2017 and 2022. Surprisingly, this segment is expanding faster than the consumer goods and services sector as a whole.[8] Although these are interesting facts, "Kink and Ink" isn't about the booming tattoo industry or who's getting beautiful butterflies or cute little kittens. On the contrary, it will serve as a savage

---

[8] Megan McCluskey, *Pandemic Woes and a 'YOLO Mentality' Have Ignited a Boom Time for Tattoo Artists,* (TIME, 2021). https://time.com/6089991/tattoo-artist-boom-covid-19/?utm_source=twitter&utm_medium=social&utm_campaign=editorial&utm_ter m=business_&linkId=129684217. Article also viewable at: dougfifer.com.

reminder of the unkind and evil aspects of human behavior. Press on at your own peril—you are now entering a universe with slightly different rules and ruthless consequences where the loss of your innocence is a foregone conclusion.

Stick and Poke . . .

The art of tattooing has been practiced by nearly every human culture since the beginning of civilization. The origins of inking can be traced back thousands of years to the Egyptian, Greek, and Roman empires. In fact, four thousand years ago, Egyptian mummies were thought to have the earliest conclusive evidence of tattooing. That is, until hikers in the Alps found a frozen corpse in the ice. This wasn't just any dead soul—it was "Ötzi the Iceman," who had sixty-one tattoos across his body.

Archaeologists used radiocarbon dating to determine the specimen's age. Remarkably, Ötzi got inked some 5,300 years ago. Without tattoo parlors or do-it-yourself ink kits, how did the Iceman get his body art? These markings were created using primitive tools such as sharpened bones or sticks. The sharp edge was used to repeatedly stick the skin, which created small incisions. Charcoal, or other natural substances, were then poked into the wound. Following this process sixty-one painful times makes Ötzi either raving mad, or one tough son of a bitch.

What kind of ink was this glacier mummy from the Copper Age (3500–2300 BC) slinging? To mention just a few, Ötzi was adorned with a bracelet-like tattoo on his wrist along with numerous horizontal and vertical lines covering most of his body. The purpose of the ancient ink is somewhat disputed by scientists. Some believe it was a form of acupuncture, while others think it was merely ornamental. Since Ötzi isn't talking, we may never know the true motivation behind his body art. One thing we do know: if Ötzi wasn't currently being displayed in a museum, the forthcoming stories of present-day tattooing would have the Iceman rolling over in his five-thousand-year-old grave.

(Discovered in the Swiss Alps in 1991)

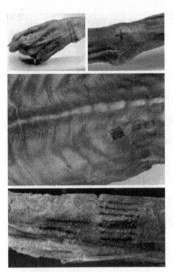

(Acupuncture or body art?)

Before we move on from the most infamous corpus delicti known to man, let's reflect upon a recent story related to Ötzi. You've probably heard the term "groupie," which refers to someone who becomes bizarrely infatuated with celebrities or rock and roll stars. In this case, we're not talking about a superfan; we're talking about a super-stalker. Some rise to the level of fanaticism by expressing their complete devotion to a person they've never met. This is common enough to be classified as an obsessive addictive disorder. As insane as it sounds, celebrity worship syndrome (CWS) does exist. Could the Iceman *possibly* have a modern-day worshipper? I introduce you to Nicole Wilson, who has curiously devoted roughly a decade to tattooing Ötzi's artwork on her very own body. Since Ötzi didn't have access to twenty-first-century ink, Nicole decided to bypass that option as well. Instead, she uses her very own blood—yes, I said blood—to recreate the markings. Although this may sound a little weird at first glance, we should probably give Nicole the benefit of the doubt. . . Okay, who in the hell are we kidding—this is full-blown batshit crazy.

In a recent article featured in *Artnet News*, Wilson speaks about her fixation with the mysterious tattoos. She chose to use blood because she wanted to mark herself with his images using something that came from her own body; this way, she believed she would literally absorb the ancient mummy's marks. Her following remark should back up my prior assumption:

"I started to become really obsessed with this idea of matching myself to history. If I could be a proxy for his body, or vice versa, what would that mean? It's about closing some kind of historical time warp, as if we could compress time."[9]

[9] Sarah Cascone, *This Is the Story of the Artist Who Has Made a Career Tattooing Herself Like Europe's Famed 'Iceman' Mummy*, (Artnet News, 2021). https://news.artnet.com/art-world/otzi-the-iceman-tattoo-show-2036395.

I hate to cherry-pick one part of the quote, but what could possibly be the significance of saying, "If I could be a proxy for his body, or vice versa, what would that mean?" Well, Nicole, it would likely mean Ötzi would be the first mummy in history to need a stalking order.[10]

The art of stick and poke is making a comeback. What was in vogue many millennia ago is now considered fashionable once again. The increasing popularity is helped by the affordability of DIY home kits, which range from fifty to seventy-five dollars. Most include needles, ink, stencils, surgical tape, and aftercare balm. Many offer instructional packets with hints and ideas for designing your tattoo. The recommendations are usually smaller in size, uncomplicated, and don't require a lot of artistic talent. Traditional body art consisting of simple lines, just like Ötzi's, is becoming more and more popular.

Alaskans, by necessity, are do-it-yourselfers. With many of our residents living remotely, being able to build and repair things comes in handy. But as we all know from personal experience, just because you can doesn't mean you should. "North to the Future" is our state's motto, meaning that Alaska is a land of promise. One thing I can promise—and the evidence will show—tattooing falls squarely within the don't-DIY category.

Marriage can be a beautiful thing, and couples on occasion share intimate tattoos to express their love. Oftentimes, they ink their partner's name, but the biggest problem here is that "until death do us part" has become a fifty-fifty shot at best. So, not surprisingly, it's the most commonly regretted design. Tattoo artists warn strongly against it, with many shops refusing to ink a lover's

---

[10] Want to see and hear Nicole for yourself? Check out the YouTube video "Linked to the Past—The Ötzi Tattoo Project": https://youtu.be/gEiA-isZ18Q. Video and article also viewable at: dougfifer.com.

name. But this didn't stop an Alaskan couple from bypassing professional interventions. With a stick-and-poke kit in hand, the
husband tattooed his own male member.

What did he tattoo? Something that proved his eternal devotion: his wife's initials on the flaccid portion of his penis. Now,
although this certainly takes guts, wouldn't her full name have
been a more powerful message? Since a cop is telling this story,
probably not. You see, the wife wasn't at all impressed with his
dick art. While at first glance this seems a little ungrateful, there's
more than meets the eye in this case.

The husband had other markings on his penis. They were all
the same: two crossed lines forming the letter X. He explained
that they were ornamental, but he also enjoyed the sensation of
adding a mark or two every so often. The wife didn't give the
admission much thought at first; after all, her initials were loud
and proud among the Xs. That is, she didn't give it much thought
until she suspected her husband of cheating. Things weren't adding up in their relationship; he would disappear at odd times,
and his excuses were revealed to be lies. At one point, while he
was at work, the wife went through his belongings. She checked
his clothes for smells, his pockets for receipts, and even the
kitchen trash for any discarded evidence. Not finding anything,
she doubted her intuition.

In a twist of fate, checking the trash would lead her to an
answer regarding her suspicion of infidelity. After searching it,
she decided to place the garbage in an outside trashcan. As she
walked past her husband's truck parked in the driveway, she
realized she hadn't searched his vehicle. He worked for a local
plumbing company, which provided a separate work vehicle. The
husband always kept his truck keys with him, but she remembered placing a spare set in a dresser drawer. Once she got in

the pickup, what she found was not at all what she expected. It wasn't a trophy pair of panties in the glove box. It wasn't a burner phone. It wasn't even a scrap of paper with a woman's number on it. While none of these would have been pleasant to find, what she did find was much worse.

A small journal was hidden at the bottom of the vehicle's center console. It was clearly her husband's handwriting, describing sexual conquest after sexual conquest—not one or two, not five or six, but eleven in total, the last of which occurred only days prior. The adulterous encounters were described in graphic sexual detail. He listed what they did, how they did it, and rated his orgasms. And the writings didn't stop there—oh, no. The pleasure seeker noted what he considered to be the crown jewel of sexual gratification: X marks the spot. The husband wanted more than just a journal entry to remember his hookups. The subsequent penile ornamental markings that began in the space after his wife's initials totaled ten. Why not eleven, as his journal documented? It seems our boy was caught prior to notching the latest fling on his ding-a-ling.

As if this wasn't traumatic enough for the wife, it got worse. The husband claimed his orgasms with his wife had intensified since the affairs. He viewed the Xs on his penis, especially when erect, as highly erotic. What really got him off was watching his wife perform oral sex while being clueless as to the meaning of the Xs. Hell hath no fury like a woman scorned, however, and in this case, it would be hard to blame the wife for seeking vengeance. She gathered up all his belongings and burned them to a crisp. Furious, he called the Anchorage Police after returning home.

Upon arrival, the wife gave me the lowdown as to how she discovered her husband's indiscretions. As proof, she read several parts of his journal aloud. She also confirmed personal knowledge of the tattoos. Obviously shocked, I asked the husband if it was his journal. "It's none of your business," was probably not the best answer, but that's what he said to me. Unbeknownst to him, he had several outstanding warrants, which I was now more than happy to assist with. Cops love karma, and every so often we get to stick it to the bad guy, who, in this case, was sticking and poking everything else, including himself.

What happened to the wife? She admitted to doing a little spring cleaning but was smart enough to say the charred remains were just a mixture of the couple's unwanted property. Without conclusive evidence, she was cited for not having a burn permit, and otherwise, the case was suspended pending new information. What about his stuff? In cop terminology, "suspended" means "zero fucks given"—without actually saying, "zero fucks given."

The Taboo Tattoo . . .

As social beings, one of our most fundamental desires is to be needed. For that reason, inking a little body art in exchange for being sexually desired might seem like a no-brainer. Even in your wildest dreams, it might be hard to imagine someone would want to fuck you solely because of your tattoo. We're not talking about a lover's name displayed on your ass, the overplayed tramp stamp, or even some sexy sleeve work.

In fact, let's take your body out of this equation and imagine a tattoo so seductive that the possessor's physical attributes simply don't matter. Too fat, too skinny, generally unattractive—not important; the ink, not your body, will put you in great demand. It's the ultimate fuck-me tattoo, and many would sell their souls for such an opportunity. But prior to making a deal with the devil, we would be wise to remember the Latin phrase *caveat emptor*—"let the buyer beware." The taboo tattoo will inevitably haunt your thoughts from here on out, because in this story, everyone gets fucked.

My law enforcement career started off fast and furious; it was pedal to the metal on crime fighting. I was a true-blue flamer, which refers to a young cop who's a little overeager while still being wet behind the ears. Veteran cops know by experience that police work is a marathon, not a sprint. I remember a rather salty old veteran telling me, "Settle down, junior, you ain't seen shit yet." I was the twenty-four-year-old new kid on the block sporting a shiny badge, polished boots, and bit of cockiness. I didn't need this crusty old bastard raining on my parade. The world was my oyster, and I was about to drop the hammer on some evildoers.

To reach the point of being a solo cop requires that you have graduated the police academy, have completed field training, and are state certified to be on your own. Most new recruits finish the academy; however, far fewer make it through field training. This is the time when senior officers, called field training officers, show you the ropes. I can tell you from personal experience that the ropes aren't pleasant. FTOs are legends in their own minds; they've seen and done it all. They are your personal drill sergeant for three painful months. I think the most heartfelt comment I received during training was, "Suck it up, buttercup." But when all was said and done, I made it through, and I was truly honored to have the opportunity to protect and serve my community.

Fast-forward a few months, and that crusty old bastard turned out to be clairvoyant. The veteran's cynical words of advice, "You ain't seen shit yet," were spot on. The truth was that my blue flame was about to be snuffed out by the dark depths of humanity. As a rookie, you get assigned the less desirable shifts coupled with the shadier parts of town. Being the low man on the totem pole, you don't question; you do as you are told. Most departments nation-wide have two cops per patrol unit, but by necessity, Anchorage is forced to lone-ranger its law enforcement duties. Geographically, Alaska and its towns are mammoth in size, so one officer per vehicle makes sense when you need to cover a large territory. Anchorage alone sprawls across 1,706 square miles, ranking it as the fourth-largest city by area in the U.S. How big is that? Really big—in fact, larger than the entire state of Rhode Island. Believe it or not, the top three metropolitan areas by landmass also belong to "America's Icebox." Texans love to say that bigger is better . . . and Alaskans couldn't agree more.

This particular Alaskan night was cold—bitterly cold, to be exact. I was assigned to an area known for heavy drug trafficking. Dealers would stand on street corners selling their dope of choice. As strange as it may seem, their lack of law-abiding behavior did not concern me nearly as much as their attire did. You might be visualizing saggy jeans, exposed underwear, and oversized hoodies. Remember, though: it's midwinter in Alaska with temperatures well below zero. They should be wearing hats, gloves, boots, and a parka, but remarkably, these street pushers would often be sporting only a light jacket, jeans, and tennis shoes.

Most of us would freeze our asses off, but they had a secret weapon against the cold: drug-induced hyperthermia, which causes the core temperature of the body to rise. Certain types of drugs, especially cocaine and amphetamines, can cause hyperthermia. This occurs when the body's heat-regulating mechanisms stop working properly and can no longer lose heat. A drug addict can be burning up inside even when it's subzero outside. If the elevated body temperature persists without medical intervention, organ failure and death can often occur. The more commonly known term, "hypothermia," is the complete opposite: the body loses heat faster than it can produce it. For example, falling into freezing water can cause hypothermia, while tweaking on crystal meth might lead to hyperthermia.

I've had to tackle a completely naked junkie, in ten-below-zero weather, running around the streets of Anchorage. He was suffering from opioid-influenced hyperthermia and would have faced certain death without police intervention. As much as it pains me to say, because of his bare-skinned jaunt, the junkie's junk suffered severe frostbite. Keep in mind that exposed skin can freeze in as little as fifteen minutes under the right conditions. Frostbite mostly affects small, exposed body parts like your fingers and toes. It's safe to say that, without clothes, he had one more "small, exposed body part" between his legs at the mercy of the elements. Since I was both unfamiliar and uncomfortable rendering first aid to his injured nether region, the package thawing was promptly turned over to medics. I did remind them that it's important to slowly and gently rewarm frostbitten areas, and they reminded me of a few four-letter words as I smiled and walked away.

It was the mid-1990s, and heroin, much like today, was widespread. My career has taught me that drugs ebb and flow almost according to fashion cycles. It's remarkably similar to clothing—simply look at the resurgence of bell-bottom jeans or Converse high-tops. Crack cocaine dominated the 1980s, disappeared for a bit, and has recently made a comeback in Alaska. Heroin, or black tar, is an opioid drug made by extracting opium from poppy plants. Afghanistan's opium harvest is estimated to account for more than 80 percent of the world's supply. Who's benefiting from such a massive crop? It's none other than the Taliban. Ironically, this Islamic fundamentalist group with close ties to al-Qaeda officially banned poppy cultivation in 2022. Prices soared after the announcement, and opium farming increased by 32 percent. The Taliban, it seems, is playing a little smoke and mirrors with the world. While the use of heroin slowed slightly in the 2000s, due to the methamphetamine explosion, it never left for good. The drug is most commonly injected with a needle, but also sniffed, smoked, or combined with other drugs. I've witnessed more heroin overdoses in my career than any other drug—simply put, it's vicious.[11]

Sadly, it is easy to identify the overdose victims of heroin and other illicit drugs. Cops call the telltale sign the "foam cone," and it looks exactly as it sounds: foaming of the mouth and nose due to the user's respiratory system shutting down. Fluids gather in

[11] United Nations Office on Drugs and Crime, *Opium Cultivation in Afghanistan*, (UNODC, 2021). https://www.unodc.org/documents/crop-monitoring/Afghanistan/Opium_cultivation_Afghanistan_2022.pdf. Article also viewable at: dougfifer.com.

the lungs, where they mix with carbon dioxide and then exit the nose and mouth, forming an intricate network of bubbles suspended in air. It's creepy the first time—every time, actually—you encounter a foam-shaped tower protruding from someone's face. The World Drug Report 2023, published by the United Nations Office on Drug and Crime, estimates sixty million people around the globe used opiate drugs for nonmedical purposes, including prescription painkillers and heroin. Additionally, more than five hundred thousand people worldwide die yearly from drug use, with opioids accounting for the majority of drug-related deaths. The U.S. has the highest overdose rate of any country. The severity of ODs becomes readily apparent when compared to the world's homicide rate, which is around 450,000 per year.[12]

Targeting everyone from street dealers to kingpins, police do everything in their power to reduce the trafficking of illegal narcotics. It's not just the DEA or undercover agents who make a difference; patrol officers play an integral role in combating drug trafficking. Looking back, I remember those dark and wintry nights when I would do my part as an Anchorage Police Officer. It was easy spotting the dealers, but it wasn't easy catching them with the actual drugs in hand. As law enforcement evolves, so too does criminal ingenuity. Street dealers know the law and find creative ways to avoid arrest. "Possession with the intent to deliver" means the drugs must be found on the suspect or be purchased in a controlled buy operation. To avoid being busted, they would often keep the heroin in their mouth and quickly swallow it upon police contact.

---

[12] United Nations Office on Drugs and Crime, *World Drug Report 2023*, (UNODC, 2023). https://www.unodc.org/res/WDR-2023/WDR23_Exsum_fin_DP.pdf. Article also viewable at: dougfifer.com.

Swallowing multiple packets of heroin is likely to cause death, so how did they do it? It was simpler than you might think. Dealers would tightly wrap the heroin in aluminum foil to avoid digestion. Upon police contact, they would swallow it, deny having any dope, and later force themselves to throw up. If arrested or detained, they would simply wait for their next bowel movement in order to have their product back. What about stomach acid? Not a problem—it doesn't dissolve aluminum, which passes undigested through your gastrointestinal tract. After a quick rinse, either way, the dealers can then put the foil-wrapped packets right back in their mouths to be sold. Dope dealing is, without question, a shitty job.

(Heroin bundles)

You've probably heard the terms "body packers" or "body stuffers," referring to people who similarly swallow their dope. This approach is slightly different in that they are usually attempting to transport drugs through airports and across borders. Put simply, body stuffers swallow narcotics for delivery to another location. Better known as "drug mules," they provide a buffer between the drug cartels and law enforcement. Think of FedEx or UPS without the planes or trucks, like an old-school, two-legged delivery service. While making some fast cash is the upside, let's not forget the number one downside of being a body packer. I don't mean the possibility of a lengthy prison sentence; as unpleasant as that may be, an even greater threat exists. Most who serve time eventually get out, but a meeting with the grim reaper leaves no second chances.

If reliable statistics existed, which they don't, this might very well be the most dangerous job on the planet. Because when the packages rupture, as they often do, death is a near certainty. These deaths are typically ruled overdoses and lack any additional investigation. If, by chance, they occur in the cartel's presence, the body is callously disposed of with a next-in-line mentality. Drug mules can be any age, but cutthroat cartels increasingly target younger victims who are less likely to attract attention. In one case, an eleven-year-old Colombian girl was found with more than one hundred cocaine capsules in her stomach. Doctors quickly operated, removed the capsules, and she was lucky enough to survive. Clint Eastwood's movie *The Mule* was based on a true story depicting the life of Leo Sharp. He was the Sinaloa Cartel's most effective drug mule at the ripe old age of eighty-seven!

The instruction manual for swallowers is short and sweet. First, some throat numbing medication which helps the smugglers swallow in excess of one hundred packages. Next, some pills are taken to prevent an untimely bowel movement. Finally, upon arrival, a laxative is taken to ensure an expeditious number two. If you aren't a big fan of shitting on demand, other options do exist.

Unlike body stuffers, body pushers skip all the above and jam-pack their vaginas or rectums. When concealed in these areas, they are usually wrapped in plastic, condoms, balloons, or latex gloves. Luckily, street cops rarely have to deal with the insertion style of concealment. It's preferable to leave the checking of vaginas to gynecologists and rectums to proctologists. Remember the slogan "Just say no to drugs" in the 1980s? I think the catchphrase could be freshened up a bit to combat public enemy number one. For instance, "Drugs have likely been in someone's ass, so how about you take a pass?" Include the following photographs, and we might finally make a dent in the war on drugs.

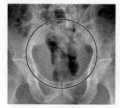 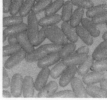 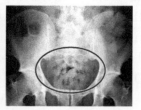

(Body packer-swallow) (Standard dope pellets)   (Body pusher rectal/
vaginal insertion)

People will go to great lengths to fulfill their addictions. Dependence on any substance, thing, or activity can be highly motivating. To understand how driven an individual can be, let's look back upon one of the strangest cases of my career. I had identified a drug peddler who was brazenly selling his product. Peddlers are typically sellers who are only working to supply their own habits. He was a white male in his mid-twenties, standing loud and proud on a notorious street corner known for dopers. He was arrogant enough to give me a friendly wave as I drove past. I was in a patrol car, full uniform, and quite easy to spot. I gave him a courtesy wave and continued driving out of sight. It's as if he didn't have a fear in the world. I was a little miffed he didn't respect the law, so it was time to show him that this rookie cop meant business.

I decided to park my police car several blocks away and double back on foot through some alleyways. It would be far more difficult for him to see this method of approach. I hid behind a nearby building and slowly peered around the corner. I saw my suspect hanging out and not really doing much of anything. After about thirty minutes, my teeth started chattering from the cold, and I decided it was time to throw in the towel. I wanted the bust oh so badly, but cold is a brutal reality check. At that very instant—and not a moment too soon—a car pulled up. The driver's side window rolled down and a prompt exchange occurred. *Sweet mother of God*, I thought, *this is my opportunity*, and I was balls to the wall after him. Unfortunately, I didn't have a plan other than grabbing him.

The car took off like a bat out of hell, and he started to run. Fortunately, I had momentum, and he was about to visit destination "fucked." A solid tackle brought us both to the ground, and before I could get the handcuffs on, he started swallowing the heroin packets. At this point, I decided screw the cuffs; I was duty bound to get the dope. I quickly pried his mouth open with both hands, which, in retrospect, was quite moronic. I had the upper part of his mouth with my left hand and the lower portion with my right. He vigorously tried to clamp down, probably not with the intention of biting me, but rather because it's nearly impossible to swallow when your jaw is forced open. At the time, little did I know, the human jaw can close teeth with a force as great as fifty-five pounds.

As I scrambled to get the upper hand, destination "fucked" was about to be reversed. I could feel my grip slipping, so I yelled, or more accurately, screamed for him to stop biting and to spit it out. If I let go, he would gulp down the goods and I wouldn't have an arrestable charge. If I tried to hold on with weakening hands, I could potentially lose a few digits. I hadn't trained for any of this, and my mind was spinning. In the police academy, you are indoctrinated with a single piece of advice, which is more powerful than anything else you learn: "When in doubt, do something." Not making a choice or freezing up in dangerous situations can have dire consequences.

Fortunately, the light bulb moment would come just in the nick of time. Cops have a powerful tool at their disposal called pepper spray. The nice thing about oleoresin capsicum (OC) is that it's nonlethal. Now, I won't minimize it too much because it does burn like hell. As I contemplated bringing the heat, it created a new dilemma. I'd need to let go of his mouth to reach my OC spray. Left with no other choice, I quickly made my move, and a split second later, I painted his face orange. Pepper spray is classified as an inflammatory agent that incapacitates the assailant. The reddish-orange color comes from its active ingredient: chili pepper resin. It immediately causes inflammation to the capillaries of the eyes and skin. Putting it mildly, you can barely breathe, barely see, and the burning is so intense, you want to vomit. Other than that, it's smooth sailing.

It worked like a charm, and my suspect started coughing and hacking, while becoming completely compliant. A couple clicks of the cuffs and the world was calm once again. Regretfully, I had not seen any signs of the dope during the struggle, and it didn't appear anything was left in his mouth. I quickly pivoted to thinking how I might eloquently document this clusterfuck in a police report when something magical happened. Remember those rather unpleasant side effects of being pepper sprayed? Our newfound right-hand man, puke, would now make a game-changing appearance. If you've ever tried to hold it in, you know it's nearly impossible. Despite his best efforts, he started violently tossing his cookies, which produced glimmers of aluminum foil hitting the ground. Without hesitation, I eagerly snatched them up, despite the intermixture of pepper spray and vomit. They say, "Beauty is in the eyes of the beholder," and at that very moment, I could not think of anything more beautiful.

The only downside to using OC is that, because of its potency, everyone nearby gets a little taste—the cop, the suspect, and pretty much anyone in the general vicinity. Fortunately, the effects only last about fifteen to twenty minutes, so recovery is quick. I was coughing a little, but my suspect bore the brunt of the discomfort. The amount of snot one human can produce after being pepper sprayed is rather remarkable. When it's cold out, the mucus partially freezes and creates snotsicles. If you think that sounds absolutely disgusting, you'd be right! To provide him with some relief, I poured a bottle of water over his eyes and face. A couple of wipes with some paper towels, and the snotsicles were gone. Yes, policing and parenting can have a lot of similarities.

I must say, it felt like Christmas came early that year. I had the heroin in hand and could prove possession. It was my first-ever possession by throwing up, but in the eyes of the law, it's solid evidence. I would charge him with misconduct involving a controlled substance and resisting arrest. The resisting comes into play since he initially ran and continued to struggle after being caught. The district attorney would later tack on a tampering with evidence charge. Why? Let's look to the law itself for the answer.

According to Alaska State Law Section 11.56.610, "a person commits the crime of tampering with physical evidence if the person destroys, mutilates, alters, suppresses, conceals, or removes physical evidence with intent to impair its verity or availability in an official proceeding or criminal investigation." Consequently, swallowing heroin packets to avoid prosecution is an attempt to destroy evidence. In rookie land, I felt like I had just taken down Pablo Escobar. The only difference was the Medellín Cartel brought in as much as $70 million per day, whereas this local level street pharmacist would be lucky to score a hundred bucks. While Escobar was undoubtedly the King of Cocaine, my guy was much closer to the bottom of the food chain.

Naivety would temporarily shield me from the reality of how powerful and unstoppable the distribution of narcotics is. The global drug trafficking market is projected at a whopping half a trillion dollars. For reference, my total take that night was six small packets containing about one-tenth of a gram each. At around 150 bucks a gram the size of a Sweet'N Low packet, I took a bush-league-level ninety dollars off the streets. Despite this inconsequential amount, I was on cloud nine after doling out a little street justice.

If you've ever heard the saying "Cops don't like paperwork," it's true. Documentation is important but quite boring for a typical adrenaline-driven officer. Nonetheless, it's essential to properly record what took place. As recently as the 1990s, the process was tedious and very slow due to handwritten reports. At the time, we didn't have the convenience of typing away at a computer keyboard. The arrest remand was in triplicates, which required pressing that pen down with some ferocity. It was very similar to the carbon copy sales receipts of yesteryear. If you didn't bear down when writing, those copies were barely legible.

The only solace was that an arrest report meant one more criminal had been taken off the streets. In this case, although the report itself wasn't unique, my suspect's answer to one question still sends chills up my spine. Name, date of birth, and address went smoothly. In hindsight, I must admit he was quite cooperative and forthcoming after our little rumble. This was a nice change of pace, as I would more typically get the customary "Go fuck yourself" from arrested suspects. But in his mind, going to jail was just part of the business. The faster he was processed in, the quicker he'd get out. Unfortunately, his attitude reflects the truth: the revolving doors of prison move at warp speed.

If you are wondering by now when the sexual aspect of this incident will come into play, it's during the Q and A. As if vomit, OC spray, snotsicles, and heroin wrapped in aluminum foil weren't enough, this fact-finding adventure was about to take an outlandish twist. One section of the report asked what I believed at the time to be a very simple, straightforward question: does the suspect have any tattoos? This is a common inquiry for identification purposes, as most tattoos are unique to the individual. Law enforcement has solved numerous crimes with the aid of ink on people's bodies. In fact, the FBI has been working closely with private industry, academia, and police departments to create a tattoo recognition database. This technology would be similar to fingerprinting and facial recognition. Tattoo tracking will certainly face some ethical oversight moving forward, but as you'll soon learn, the upside is not to be shrugged at.

Before we get into the explosive revelation from my suspect, let's look at an actual homicide solved by a seemingly inconsequential ink design. In 2004, an assassination-style murder occurred outside of a neighborhood liquor store in California. Authorities theorized it was likely a gang-related shooting, but witnesses would not come forward because they feared retaliation. The case would go cold for four years until police stopped a motorist for driving with a suspended license. The driver, Anthony Garcia, was reputed to be an active member of the notorious Rivera-13 gang.

Los Angeles, nicknamed the "gang capital of America," is estimated to have 450 active street gangs comprising more than forty-five thousand members. LAPD officially recorded 16,398 verified gang crimes over their last three-year reporting period. These include 491 homicides, roughly 7,047 felony assaults, approximately 5,518 robberies, and nearly one hundred sexual assaults. Curiously, these statistics are more than a few years old and are not consistently updated. It is difficult to ascertain exact numbers as police departments across our nation are continuously under pressure to reduce crimes. Figures are often categorized differently to achieve the appearance of a lower crime rate. The sad reality is that politics play a role in policing. One thing we do know is that, as of 2022, current LAPD gang-related homicides represent more than half of all murders in Los Angeles. Despite recategorizing criminal offenses, it appears gangs are still raining terror upon society.

The Rivera-13 gang, founded in the early 1960s, takes orders from the Mexican Mafia. By adding the number 13 to their name, Rivera demonstrates that allegiance. The Mexican Mafia is often referred to as "*la eMe*," which is Spanish for the letter M, the thirteenth letter of the alphabet. Think of it as giving your middle name to your son or daughter. It's a sign of love and respect (but without the murder and mayhem thrown in for good measure). The Mexican Mafia is a long-standing U.S. criminal organization with territory in California and throughout the U.S. federal prison system. It originated in the 1950s to protect its members from other prison gangs. The members honor a strict hierarchy with a written constitution outlining every aspect of the criminal organization. *La eMe* also has a "blood in, blood out" credo—this means that murdering or drawing blood is the only way in, and death is the only way out.

While prominent in the prison system, their status and reputation reach far beyond the walls of the penitentiary. The Mexican Mafia actively engages in narcotics, murder, money laundering, kidnapping, human trafficking, illegal gambling, and anything else that bolsters their organization. Like any successful business, they operate with a specific set of guidelines and rules. They are also heavily engaged in homosexual prostitution within the prison system. The irony here is that their constitution doesn't allow fellow gang members to be homosexual. Even more perplexing is that, like pimps, they occasionally sample the goods. We'll get into more specifics in a bit, but for now it seems that rules are made to be broken.

Look at the Mexican Mafia's rules of conduct below and pay particular attention to the sixth rule, which refers to their prohibition against homosexuality.

1. A member may not be an informant.

2. A member may not be a coward.

3. A member may not raise a hand against another member without approval from the higher-ups and leaders.

4. A member must not show disrespect for any member's family, including sex with another member's wife or girlfriend.

5. A member must not steal from another member.

6. A member may not be homosexual, a sex offender, child killer, child molester, or rapist.

7. A member must not politic against another member or cause dissension within the organization.

8. Membership is for life; the only way out is death.

9. Retaliation must be carried out if anyone crosses *La eMe*—no exceptions.

10. Vendetta must be carried out, even if it takes months, years, or decades.

11. If a member of *La eMe* gets harmed or killed by someone else such as police or another criminal gang, retaliation must be immediate, and must be swift, brutal, and deadly.

12. It's mandatory to assault/kill all dropouts and traitors.

13. *La eMe* comes first. Even before your own family, religion, and God.

14. A member must not interfere with another member's business activities.

15. A member must never harm children.

16. A member must always treat another member's family with respect and kindness.

17. A member must protect another member from harm.

18. A member must treat another member like a brother.

While I wouldn't go as far as becoming a blood-in associate of the Mexican Mafia, the latter part of the sixth rule forbidding sex offenders, child killers, child molesters, or rapists makes a lot of sense. But let's get back to the elephant in the room: the prohibition against homosexuality. The Mexican Mafia has a peculiar version of moral high ground, which certainly requires some additional context. How could this gigantic paradox, in which imprisoned homophobes operate and partake in homosexual prostitution, possibly connect to a small-time Alaskan dope peddler? Trust me, we'll come full circle on this one, but for now, let's add a few things to this thought-provoking contradiction.

What do a suspended license, tattoo, murder, sexual orientation, Alaska, heroin, and the Mexican Mafia have in common? It turns out, more than you might think—a lot more. It all starts with that earlier traffic stop involving gang member Anthony Garcia. From there, the events would lead investigators down an unusual path. Customarily, police take photographs of tattoos during an arrest. This is especially true when it comes to gangbangers. It is an additional way to confirm suspected gang membership, as members often proudly display proof of loyalty to their respected gang on their skin. This will play a role in Anthony Garcia's arrest, and you will begin to marvel at Garcia's dubious mental acuity; although still living, he undoubtedly deserves to be an honorary recipient of the Darwin Award.

Twenty-three-year-old John Juarez was standing in front of a local liquor store when he was gunned down by Anthony Garcia. Juarez was murdered simply because he belonged to a rival gang. As is common in gang killings, witnesses refuse to testify, and cops have very little to go on. The FBI puts the national solve rate for murders just above 50 percent. But if you separate out the gang killings, the solve rate plummets to well below 30 percent.[13] I guess we now know where the saying "getting away with murder" comes from. Why are witnesses so reluctant to cooperate with authorities? The United States Constitution, specifically the Sixth Amendment, allows a person accused of a crime to confront a witness in court. Gangs take advantage of this by paying a visit to your family circle and delivering the following daunting message: "Say one word and we'll kill each and every one of you." Testifying at one's own peril is bad enough, but doing it at the peril of your entire family makes turning a blind eye to murder the only option.

In the case of Anthony Garcia, a witness did talk, and quite literally spilled the beans. Who among us would have the courage to stand up against such evil? Who would openly defy intimidation without fear of reprisal? And most importantly, how would authorities corroborate the evidence provided? As luck would have it, the crime scene would be flawlessly mapped out for them. The witness proved his reliability, because without firsthand knowledge of the crime, this would not have been possible. He described the liquor store, the position of the victim, the trajectory of the bullets, and even why the homicide was committed. The informer also knew that Anthony Garcia referred to his victim as Mr. Peanut, a derogatory name for a rival gang. He knew that Garcia, who went by the street name "Chopper," had proudly and openly acknowledged the fact that he had riddled the peanut with bullets to reclaim Rivera-13's turf.

This was enough information to convict Garcia of first-degree murder, leading to a sixty-five-year prison sentence. To whom should we express our gratitude for removing Garcia from the

---

[13] Tyler Wornell, *Nearly half of US murders going unsolved, data show*, (NewsNation, 2023). https://www.newsnationnow.com/crime/us-murder-clearance-rate-decline/. Article also viewable at: dougfifer.com.

public gene pool? You might not believe it, but the witness turned out to be Mr. Garcia himself, and he didn't have to say a word. Somewhere there's a village—or in this case a gang—missing its idiot, and if you look at the photographs below, you'll quickly come to realize how this silent witness revealed everything.

(Booking Photo)   (Crime scene tattoo)

Yes, seeing is believing. He physically tattooed the complete crime scene on his chest. Garcia's eye for detail was remarkable. He included the liquor store, complete with Christmas lights that were still hanging when the murder occurred. He added a nearby light pole with street signs. Perhaps the most sinister part of the rendering is a peanut being riddled with bullets by a menacing helicopter. Garcia's arrogance was undeniable: the helicopter was an homage to his nickname "Chopper." To make it perfectly clear what the illustration depicted, he adorned the top of the tattoo with an explanatory caption. It proudly boasted, "Rivera kills."

Anthony Garcia avoided arrest for four years until that fateful traffic stop in 2008. Had he not been so brazen with his body art, it is very likely he would have never answered for this crime. Brock Lunsford, the deputy district attorney at the time, prosecuted the case and called the ill-famed tattoo a "nonverbal confession." We should give a special shout-out to now-retired Los Angeles County Sheriff's Homicide Detective Sergeant Kevin Lloyd. While looking through photographs of gang member's tattoos, he remembered the murder scene depicted on Garcia's chest. Sergeant Lloyd had previously worked for the Pico Rivera Sheriff's Station and responded in 2004 to the homicide. This improbable twist of fate was one in a million, and without Lloyd, nobody would be cashing in that lotto ticket. Fortunately for our communities, incredible work is done every day by the men and women in law enforcement.

Up to this point, we have pretty much covered the gamut on all things tattoo related. We've touched on sexual seduction, Ötzi the Iceman, penis poking, the Mexican Mafia, and a rival gang murder, just to name a few. To bring it all home, let's get back to that cold wintry night in Anchorage. Remember: our low-level street pusher had a specific question to answer regarding tattoos. His subsequent disclosure will reveal the most gut-wrenching body art in the history of mankind.

Our conversation went something like this:

ME: Do you have any tattoos?

SUSPECT: Yeah, I do.

ME: Where is it located?

SUSPECT: On my back.

ME: What is it?

SUSPECT: It's a female.

ME: Who's the female?

SUSPECT: It's a prison tat.

ME: Okay, is it of your girlfriend or mom?

SUSPECT: No! It's a prison tat of a woman.

ME: I get that part; it was done in prison, but who is it?

SUSPECT: Are you fucking kidding me? Are you a rookie?

At the moment, I wasn't tracking the handwriting on the wall. When street thugs call you a rookie, it pisses you off. It's their not-so-subtle way of mocking you for your inexperience. Obviously, despite my best efforts, my greenness was still quite evident. Since he was the one in handcuffs in my back seat, I wasn't too offended. I reminded him he was the experienced dealer who was going to jail. If he didn't want to tell me about the tattoo, I'd simply have the jailers strip off his shirt and fill in the blanks from there.

Back to our conversation:

SUSPECT: You really don't know what a prison tat is?

ME: Like I said, it doesn't matter.

SUSPECT: It's of a female that covers my entire back.

ME: I get it, someone tattooed you in prison.

SUSPECT: You don't get it.

ME: I'm not going to play a guessing game, so just tell me who the woman is.

SUSPECT: The woman isn't anybody.

ME: We're done talking since you're fucking with me now.

SUSPECT: It's so when you have sex in prison, you aren't gay.

At this point in the conversation, we were driving to the jail. Did I hear that last part right? Could I have misheard him? Or maybe he was trying to bait me into looking stupid. I played it cool, calm, and collected. I kept driving, even though my mind was reeling.

> SUSPECT: You don't know what I'm talking about, do you?
>
> ME: I guess I don't.
>
> SUSPECT: It's of a woman with long hair, tits, and a pussy.
>
> ME: Why would you have that tattooed on your back?
>
> SUSPECT: (*Nonchalantly*) The pussy is my asshole.
>
> ME: You can't be serious.
>
> SUSPECT: Like I said, it's so when men have sex with me, they aren't gay. They're fantasizing about the tattoo.
>
> ME: Rookie or not, I'm calling bullshit.
>
> SUSPECT: No bullshit, and I'm not gay either; it's about survival.

As we pulled up to the jail, I genuinely didn't know what to believe. This guy was almost too matter-of-fact in describing what would normally be a truly horrific set of circumstances. I mean, when someone says out loud, "The pussy is my asshole," that's a pretty big matzo ball hanging out there to ignore. I felt strangely compelled to investigate further—just not in the touchy-feely kinda way.

The process for booking someone into jail is simple. The police officer gives the jailer the required paperwork, including the arrest remand, and they take custody of the prisoner. I explained to the corrections officer that my suspect was claiming to have some rather unique body art, and before I could accurately document it, I'd need to have a quick look. Correctional facilities operate with a different set of rules than cops. They pretty much have carte blanche in searching anyone that enters. As expected, the CO was not in any mood to mess around. He told my suspect to strip off his clothes, and without hesitation, that's exactly what he did.

Staring at this naked man's backside would be a defining moment in my career. In an instant, my world forever changed. Before my very own eyes was a tattoo so remarkable, it was almost inconceivable to mentally accept. It was exactly how my suspect had described it. What blew my mind was the artistry of the image; it was incredibly detailed and genuinely looked like a woman. The hair was long and flowing, encompassing both sides of the back, neck, and arms. The face looked directly at me, the eyes so realistic, I felt awkward looking back at them. I remember the slender eyebrows and dainty nose above a pair of voluminous lips. *This couldn't be real*, I kept thinking, and if there was ever a time I needed a safe space, it was at this moment.

It was like a car crash I couldn't look away from. You don't want to stare, but you can't help yourself. As if a feminine face wasn't compelling enough, the rest of the tattoo would elevate it to another level: perfectly symmetrical breasts, worthy of a board-certified plastic surgeon, were positioned at the midpoint of the back. The shadowing details of the ink made them appear three-dimensional, almost as if they were sitting on top of the skin. The areolae and nipples only enhanced the realness. How could a tattoo be so lifelike and detailed?

Tattoos are two-dimensional images, but by adding highlights and shading techniques, the artist can create a 3D optical illusion. It takes incredible skill and years of experience to master such eye-popping designs. In the dealer's case, the sides of his lower back were shaded to highlight the hips, giving them a curvier appearance. Incredibly, the larger breasts in proportion to the thin waist created an hourglass figure. Okay, stay with me, people—it's too late to turn back now. We must finish what we've started. Truth be told, describing this is as therapeutic for me as it is distressing for you. Not to be blunt, but the pussy/asshole were interchangeable in their shared location. The vertical line dividing his left and right ass cheeks was the start of a full bush leading down to his "prison pocket." To be fair, I did warn you that some of the things you read and see in these pages you'll never be able to unread or unsee.

We've all heard that addicts need to hit rock bottom before they get help, and whether that's true or not in general, this poor bastard couldn't possibly get any lower. If this had happened today, I would have started a GoFundMe campaign for his laser tattoo removal. I have little doubt his taboo tattoo would have broken records for crowdfunding.

Cops will often use a basic information-gathering set of questions called the Five Ws: the who, what, when, where, and why of an investigation. In this case, I should have wanted to find out where the dealer got the dope or who he was selling it to. I still needed to answer some of the Five Ws, only now, I was less interested in the criminal charges. In truth, I had become strangely preoccupied with a heroin addict's backside. Legally, he was under no obligation to cooperate, but he freely agreed to talk about it. The questioning was not meant in any way to disparage or make light of his circumstances, as I genuinely felt bad for him. After hearing his complete life story, I believed he deserved a stint in rehab rather than jail.

The "why" was because of a heroin habit, which he referred to as smack. He told me about his first time using it when he was fifteen years old and living in California. It was the greatest high of his life, and from that day forward, he thought of nothing else. Within the first month of using the drug, he was stealing from his parents. Within six months, he had dropped out of high school, becoming homeless and an easy target for predators. His cravings only grew stronger, and desperately in need of money, he turned to unsavory acts. Again, and without provocation, he insisted he wasn't gay. And if I ever became "dope sick," I'd understand exactly what he meant. The physical withdrawal symptoms were so severe, he would do anything for the next fix. He summed up his total dependence on the drug by saying, "I'd rather die than go without."

Heroin or death is a choice most of us, thankfully, will never have to make. It's difficult for nonaddicts to fathom what could possibly make the risk of death preferable to abstinence. We've already illustrated the devastating repercussions from using heroin, but how you ingest the dope can greatly precipitate this downward spiral. A common method involves heating the heroin on aluminum foil with a lighter. The resulting vapor is then inhaled, which rapidly enters the brain and binds to opioid receptors. These receptors regulate pain, hormone release, and feelings of euphoria. They also target the reward center of the brain. So how good is a heroin high? I asked our suspect this very question, and his response was startling. He told me to think about the greatest sexual orgasm of my life and multiply it by a hundred. Can you imagine humanity's sexual cravings increasing a hundredfold? It would be total chaos on planet Earth. Forget about the zombie apocalypse; the forthcoming porn apocalypse would literally fuck civilization to death.

(Chasing the dragon)

So why is inhaling the most addictive and potentially lethal method of using heroin? Users call it "chasing the dragon," and it wreaks total havoc on your brain. The term comes from the smoke created by heating the drug; it slowly rises from the aluminum foil and moves around like a Chinese dragon dancing. For users, it's the ultimate high, but with dire consequences. Using heroin in any manner is risky business, but inhaling the drug causes toxic leukoencephalopathy, a disease that damages the white matter in your brain, resulting in sponge-like tissue. Think of your brain looking like Swiss cheese, with the connectivity disrupted and normal mental functions lost. Scientific studies have proven that chasing the dragon harms the brain significantly more than any other method of ingestion.

Let's get back to my arrest and subsequent discovery of the taboo tattoo. We know now that heroin was the why, but we still have the who, what, when, and where to answer. For most of you, the preceding information was likely shocking enough, but the following history will be nearly incomprehensible. After floating on the streets for many years, he started selling heroin to support his habit. He was arrested several times, which led to longer and longer stints in jail. He must have thought it was amateur hour when I asked how it was possible that he didn't get dope sick in jail. Quite confidently, he said, "I can get smack anytime and anywhere I'm locked up." On the streets, heroin has hundreds of names, but "smack" seems to be the go-to slang term for addicts. As a new cop, it didn't seem possible to me that jail was a one-stop shop for dope. After twenty-five years on the job, I now know truer words have never been spoken. Anything you can get on the outside—and I mean *anything* at all—is readily available on the inside.

Slowly but surely, as he worked his way through the court system, he earned some real time in one of America's most notorious prisons: San Quentin, a maximum-security correctional facility located near San Francisco. Opened in 1854, it is California's oldest penitentiary. If you've ever watched the TV documentary *Lockup*, you have probably noticed that the series regularly features San Quentin inmates. The prison has housed some of the most savage killers on the planet. Two of the most infamous were Charles Manson and Richard Ramirez, also known as "The Night Stalker," who, combined, killed over twenty people. San Quentin is, quite frankly, a gated community of serial killers. It houses the majority of death row criminals in California and has the largest death row population in America. It is one of the most violent and feared incarceration facilities the world has ever known.

Drug smuggling into prisons, especially San Quentin, is far-reaching and nonstop. Law enforcement has arrested staff, visitors, and even sworn correctional officers attempting to get illegal narcotics to inmates. Although trafficking includes the complete spectrum of drugs, heroin remains king. Prison gangs can make upwards of a $1,000 for each gram. As mentioned earlier, with a street cost of around $150, that's some serious profit. The drug trade in prison is so prolific that gangs use correctional officers and employees for what they call "stash smuggling." The Mexican Mafia has an actual recruitment team that flashes money to catch the interest of susceptible staff. They derogatorily use the term "cowboy" when targeting a new correctional officer—spelled backwards, it means, "young, obnoxious, bastard we often con."

Profit drives the discovery of new marks and innovative ways to run contraband, including the use of technology. In a recent 2021 case at another California lockup facility, a drone was used to smuggle in Xanax, methamphetamine, muscle relaxers, and, of course, heroin. Money is power in the free world, but it's doubly so in the penitentiary. The black market in San Quentin, for example, is so severe, the FBI maintains an ongoing probe in an effort to combat these activities. In 2021 at San Quentin, Keith Christopher, a prison guard, was charged with smuggling cellphones to death row inmates. The trafficking of cell phones might appear to be rather harmless, but they can be far more lethal than drugs. Imprisoned gang leaders use these phones to run drug rackets, orchestrate murders, and facilitate the influx of contraband into correctional institutions. The Mexican Mafia wields power far beyond the prison walls. Think back to Anthony Garcia, a.k.a. "Chopper"—he wasn't a shot caller, so his order to kill was likely sanctioned by leadership within the prison walls.

If slinging dope on the inside and out, arranging murders, and having correctional officers on the payroll weren't bad enough, let's look at the prison sex trade. Pimping out inmates is a specialty of the Mexican Mafia; they brazenly run business-like brothels behind bars. How do they get away with this? It's because sex crimes are so widespread throughout penitentiaries that the sheer numbers, combined with a lack of cooperation, makes them nearly impossible to investigate. It's important to remember that victims are highly unlikely to report due to the number one cardinal rule in prison: no snitching. If reporting meant your life, you're probably going to keep your mouth shut.

Regardless, the California prison system is legally required to investigate and report all sexual crimes related to inmates. They are categorized into five classifications:

1. Inmate-on-inmate nonconsensual acts
2. Inmate-on-inmate abusive sexual contact
3. Inmate-on-inmate sexual harassment
4. Staff-on-inmate sexual misconduct
5. Staff-on-inmate sexual harassment

Each report further subdivides these crimes into substantiated, unsubstantiated, unfounded, or as part of an ongoing investigation.

Let's look more closely at the official language describing the first item in the list. Inmate-on-inmate nonconsensual sex acts is defined as "contact of an offender by another offender without his or her consent, or by coercion; or contact of an offender who is unable to consent or refuse and contact between the penis and vagina or the penis and anus including penetration, however slight; or contact between the mouth and the penis, vagina, or anus or penetration of the anal or genital opening of another person by the hand, finger, or other object."

The combined number of sexual assault allegations in California prisons for 2022 totaled 1,279. The California prison population has fluctuated over the last several years but remains around 115,000 to 125,000 inmates. If the numbers were accurate, we'd be led to believe sexual violence only affects about 1 percent of the population, although this seems like a gross underestimate. To make this even more vague and implausible, that percentage would mean that every allegation had also been substantiated, when in fact, the vast majority are not. The California Department of Corrections and Rehabilitation (CDCR) states it has zero tolerance for sexual abuse and diligently investigates all allegations. Clearly, organized prison prostitution alone makes this hard to fathom. The reported numbers, therefore, are truly laughable, and the Mexican Mafia laugh all the way to the bank.[14]

---

[14] *Prison Rape Elimination Act Annual Report—Calendar Year 2022*, (California Department of Corrections and Rehabilitation, 2023). https://www.cdcr.ca.gov/prea/wp-content/uploads/sites/186/2023/08/Annual-PREA-Report-Calender-Year-2022.pdf. Article also viewable at: dougfifer.com.

So, what are the real numbers? These violent acts, as one would expect, are not unique to California's prison system. U.S. penitentiaries are plagued with a vicious cycle of predatory behavior. In 2003, Congress signed into law the Prison Rape Elimination Act. Supporting documentation noted that insufficient research had been conducted and little data gathered on the full extent of prison rape. It was also conservatively estimated by experts that at least 13 percent of inmates in the US have been sexually assaulted in prison. If we take 2023's total U.S. incarcerated population, which hovers around two million, we can presume that more than 250,000 inmates have been or will be the victims of prison rape. The report also mentioned that young, first-time offenders are at a higher risk and are often assaulted within forty-eight hours of imprisonment.[15]

What does this mean for the CDCR's numbers? It suggests they are woefully low. Using the 13 percent figure, we end up with more than fifteen thousand sexual assaults just within the Golden State's prison system. This certainly demonstrates the effect of that number one cardinal rule: snitches get stitches. With these numbers, Congress further established that the high sexual assault rate within prisons involves actual and potential violations of the U.S. Constitution. There is legal precedent—in 1994, the Supreme Court ruled, under Farmer v. Brennan, that deliberate indifference to the substantial risk of sexual assault violates prisoners' rights under the Cruel and Unusual Punishment Clause of the Eighth Amendment.[16]

---

[15] Wendy Sawyer and Peter Wagner, *Mass Incarceration: The Whole Pie 2023*, (Prison Policy Initiative, 2023). https://www.prisonpolicy.org/reports/pie2024.html.

[16] Check out the ruling for yourself: https://supreme.justia.com/cases/federal/us/511/825/case.pdf.

Articles also viewable at: dougfifer.com.

As for our drug-dealing suspect in Anchorage, heroin addiction wasn't the full extent of the why. The reason for his taboo tattoo was because it was the only solution, albeit quite cruel, for surviving in a predatory environment. The Mexican Mafia had targeted him for exploitation from the moment he arrived. They freely provided heroin with an agreement to settle up later. When the time came and he couldn't pay, he was given two choices: they would beat him to death, or he could work as a prison prostitute. Providing sexual services would also guarantee his future rations of dope. He learned that three types of sexual preferences existed in prison: homosexuals, heterosexuals, and prison wolves. A prison wolf is a male who stays straight on the outside but engages in sexual activity with men while incarcerated. By rule, a Mexican Mafia member must remain heterosexual, so aside from masturbation, getting one's rocks off in prison isn't an option—that is, unless you tattoo a beautiful woman on a man's backside, which then makes fucking him perfectly okay. Now, before the Mexican Mafia sanctions a hit on me, I say to them, "Don't shoot the messenger boys. I give you full credit for finding a way around rule number six." Because in all fairness, that must have been a tough nut to crack!

Given the artistry of our suspect's back tat, it somehow seems oddly fitting that Leonardo da Vinci enters the picture at this point. Among the greatest painters ever known, da Vinci's influence has been considerable throughout art history. But could da Vinci have inspired a heroin addict's taboo tattoo some five hundred years ago? By way of explanation, it's important to note that the Italian Renaissance artist studied anatomical models to perfect his art of creating lifelike images. Da Vinci boldly broke from traditional chaste practices by creating what were considered at the time to be flirtatious portraits. His most famous work, the *Mona Lisa*, is considered a timeless masterpiece. She displays a playful smile coupled with seductive eyes, and her image is far and away the most visited painting in the world. Housed at the Louvre in Paris, you'll pay about fifteen euros (seventeen U.S. dollars) to spend a few moments together. As unlikely as it may seem, the taboo tattoo and the *Mona Lisa* share some unique commonalities.

It might, at first glance, seem implausible to make a comparison between the two. But if you really think about it, you'll appreciate their similarities. Knowing that creating such a true-to-life tattoo takes extraordinary talent, then perhaps the Mexican Mafia diligently studied da Vinci's technique; either that, or his bloodline found its way into the prison system some twenty generations later. Like the *Mona Lisa*, the taboo tattoo was anatomically correct and undoubtedly took time to perfect. The artist, like da Vinci, boldly broke from traditional practices. As for being a timeless masterpiece, will you ever forget my description of it? With her seductively enhanced qualities, she, too, was far and away the most visited artwork at her respective museum: in this case, San Quentin. As with da Vinci's painting, you'd also pay about twenty dollars to spend a few moments in her company.

The similarities end there. Unlike the *Mona Lisa*, the taboo tattoo was all about fantasy—pretending to achieve a "happy ending."

Ballsy Body Art . . .

Being lightheaded and weak in the knees is never a good look for a cop. We are taught to stay in control of the situation, no matter how bad it gets. This composure is usually a tried-and-true formula for when shit hits the fan. It's a rare occasion when the shock value is so great that you can barely speak and feel like fainting. Being silent and dizzy is also frowned upon in law enforcement, especially since you carry a loaded handgun along with other weapons. For the first time in my career, on one occasion, I had to lean against the wall and eventually sit down. I was dizzy, my vision closing in, and I felt sick to my stomach. Imagine calling 911 for help, and I show up as a soup sandwich.

I told myself to breathe slowly, in and out. I remember asking a completely naked female for water. A clock was ticking on the wall, so I focused on that instead of the agonizing screams of pain around me. I repeated a mantra internally: "It will be okay. It will be okay." While these words are normally intended for whoever is suffering, I couldn't get past the trauma of what I was seeing enough to help anyone. My Achilles' heel had been revealed, but enough about my first-time panic attack—let's get back to the nude woman and bloodcurdling shrieks for help.

When the call originally came in, it was initially dispatched as a standard medical assist. The person told the dispatcher that her boyfriend was injured, and they needed medical attention fast. She was freaking out and didn't relay exactly what the problem was. Dispatch was able to ascertain that it was not a case of domestic violence, nor was the injury life threatening. Nine times out of ten, calls like these go something like this:

1. Cop shows up.

2. Nobody is dead.

3. Cop turns it over to medics.

On this occasion, it went more like this:

1. Cop shows up.

2. Cop nearly passes out.

3. Medics end up trying to help cop.

Now before you unfairly judge me, I should say that I do have a respectable excuse. It all started with a game affectionately called "punish the penis." While this might sound like a guy being cut off from sex, the truth is, it's far from it. In practice, this game is a form of foreplay during which the male finds pleasure in pain. Prior to my arrival, we had two partners consensually engaging in sadomasochistic erotic play. This wasn't your conventional *Fifty Shades of Grey* style of S&M, however; this was leveling up. Sorry, Christian Grey, but hair pulling, flogging, spanking, and biting nipples wouldn't even come close to getting this guy off.

Before we get into the meat of this story, I should mention that my earlier dizziness subsided a few minutes after seeing the sex-related injury, so I was back in action pretty quickly. The water helped, and looking back, this might have been the only time I've asked for a drink from someone in crisis. It was certainly the only time I've received water from a naked stranger. Why was she *au naturel*? It turns out the two were having some rather unusual rough sex, which led to a gruesome injury. The female remained in such shock that she didn't think about getting dressed before I arrived. In my twenty-five years of experience, I have seen nearly every injury imaginable: oozing gunshot wounds, limbs cut off, and eyes gouged out. None of it held a candle to this trauma. The male had a broken penis, more commonly known as a penile fracture.

Cops are taught to do a quick primary assessment when encountering an injured person. In this case, I didn't need to do the ABCs (airway, breathing, and circulation). He was writhing in pain, yelling, "Help me," and erratically jumping around. It's hard to do this without breathing or having a heartbeat, so I checked those concerns off the list. Next up was a secondary survey to determine the history of the incident, examine the injury, and check vital signs. The male was not in any shape to give me the background, so instead, I asked to take a closer look at the damaged area. He was naked as well, except for an ice pack and small hand towel covering his crotch. When he pulled them away, I spontaneously said, "Oh my God."

What I saw was the cause of my earlier wooziness. It was a massively swollen penis, bent nearly sideways, and dark purple in color. The tip had blood leaking out, and the scrotum was greenish black. The only other times I had seen this color on a body part was from gangrene. I quickly asked the girlfriend to verify if the injury was recent, as his ball sack shouldn't have been anywhere close to its current color. She confirmed it had just happened and followed up with "His balls are tattooed so that part is normal." It was at this moment when I realized both the male and female were almost entirely tatted from head to toe. As unlikely as it may seem, in the commotion, I somehow missed this despite them being naked. Although I had more questions, I first thought to myself, *Who in the hell inks their balls?* And her nonchalant reference to it, suggesting its normality, really threw me for a loop. I have testicles, and the skin around them is soft and sensitive, so just thinking about the intense pain involved in getting my scrotum tattooed makes me queasy.

Minutes felt like hours until medics arrived. Once there, they did a proper examination and started readying the male for a ride to the hospital. He had calmed slightly but was still in obvious pain. They asked the female what happened, and she told them, "His penis accidentally got jammed during sex." As the medics were about to leave, she unfortunately had one more tidbit to tell: "Are you going to check on the policeman since he almost passed out?" I thought to myself, *Come on, lady. This isn't good for my reputation.* I could see the amused, wide eyes of medics as they turned toward me and sarcastically asked, "Shall we get a gurney for you too?" They cheekily added, "Would you like us to check your blood sugar?" I think of it as payback—I was getting a little bit of my own medicine. After declining help, I told them to get going since someone else's manhood was literally at risk.

After reminding her to get dressed, I interviewed the female and found out her boyfriend was a local tattoo artist. They co-owned a prominent shop in Anchorage that had been in business for many years. In fact, many of my police counterparts had received their sleeve work there. She continued by saying that most of the ink canvassing their bodies was done by her partner. I had to ask why he had tattooed his balls. Without hesitation she explained, "His penis was also tattooed, but it was probably difficult for you to see due to the injury." When I expressed how painful it must have been, she interjected, "We both like a little pain in our game," and followed up with, "My clit has some ink as well." Usually, I like to build up to uncomfortable questions, but it wasn't necessary in this case. While I wasn't touching the clit remark, I did need to find out what happened. Here's how the Q and A went:

ME: I know you mentioned sex to the medics, but can you tell me how the injury occurred?

HER: I was tattooing his balls and he pushed me off.

ME: Wait, I thought he did the tattooing? And how did he push you off?

HER: He does the professional tattooing, but we also ink each other. I was riding him, facing away (*reverse cowgirl*), and the pain was too much.

ME: The pain from riding him?

HER: No, the pain from tattooing.

ME: Okay, I'm not quite following here.

HER: (*points to a tattoo gun on a nearby table*) I was using that to tattoo his balls while having sex.

ME: While you were having sex?

HER: Yes, he likes physical pain and pleasure at the same time.

ME: How did the accident happen?

HER: He couldn't take the pain anymore, so he tried to push me off. It slipped out while I was going up and down. As I came back down, I felt it hit my pubic bone and heard a popping sound.

ME: And while you were going up and down you were still tattooing?

HER: Yes, I was bent over, leaning forward.

ME: Did he ask you to stop what you were doing at any time?

HER: No, he just tried to lift me off. We've done the same thing many times before. It's a game we play.

ME: A game?

HER: He calls it "punish the penis." That's his thing: he likes his genitals abused.

ME: Do you tattoo his penis as well?

HER: I have, but he can't perform when that happens.

ME: (*silently thinking in my mind, I couldn't either!*)

I find myself needing to take a deep breath once again after writing this. They say a broken heart is one of the worst feelings, but I think a broken penis tops it. BDSM (bondage, discipline or domination, submission or sadism, masochism) is more common than you might think. A 2023 study found 42.4 percent of Americans report trying BDSM at one point, while 34 percent participate on a regular basis.[17] It's not just the U.S.—a Belgian study in *The Journal of Sexual Medicine* reports that 46.8 per-

---

[17] Bedbible Research Center, *BDSM Statistics—How Common Is BDSM? Facts, Stats and Complete Info*, (Bedbible 2023). https://bedbible.com/bdsm-statistics-facts-stats/. Article also viewable at: dougfifer.com.

cent of the sample size had performed at least one BDSM-related activity, while 12.5 percent indicated they engage in this as a regular behavior. So, who's the kinkiest country when it comes to BDSM play?[18] It's hard to say for certain, but Belgium and the U.S. statistically love this kind of foreplay. If you are thinking these percentages can't be possible, just remember the *Fifty Shades of Grey* trilogy has sold over 150 million copies worldwide.

While a little tie-up session and dirty talk sound nice, a piercing needle to the genitals does not. Don't get me wrong. I'm good with padded handcuffs and soft spanking—even tickling with a feather sounds pleasurable—but inking my junk is a no-go. Cock and ball torture falls squarely within the sadomasochism (S&M) category of BDSM. In a nutshell, players of this game inflict or receive physical or psychological pain to derive pleasure. If you are wondering what common types of cock and ball torture exist? Here is a list:

- **Testicle crushing.** This one has a few options. You can simply use your hand to control the crush, but if you want to take it up a notch, you can purchase sex toys called ball crushers or nutcrackers. Amazon currently sells a penis and testicle crusher for under forty bucks.

- **Testicle stretching.** This can be achieved by pulling the testicles forcibly away from the body. Some attach a ring and weight for better results. You can buy the Master Series custom ball stretcher kit online for under twenty dollars.

---

[18] Lien Holvoet, et al, *Fifty Shades of Belgian Gray: The Prevalence of BDSM-Related Fantasies and Activities in the General Population*, (The Journal of Sexual Medicine 14, no. 9, 2017). https://academic.oup.com/jsm/article-abstract/14/9/1152/6973476. Article also viewable at: dougfifier.com.

- **Penis trampling.** Ouch, it's just as it sounds. Someone steps or stomps on your penis. This one doesn't have a specific product to assist. It's more of a hands-on service you'll need to pay for.

- **Penis flogging and wax play.** Flogging is the use of a whip or paddle to inflict pain, while wax play involves dripping hot, melted wax onto the genitals. Yes, a starter kit exists with instructional videos as well.

- **Erotic electrostimulation.** This involves direct application of electrodes to the genitals. While some like a gentle, tickle-like buzz, others prefer a hardcore zapping. You can get the best of both worlds by purchasing a Volt Electro-Charge. It has five levels of electrostimulation and advertises itself as being "shockingly good." Even better, it's rechargeable and affordable. Frying your junk has a sixty-dollar price tag.

- **Urethra play.** While I'm not doing any of the above, this one brings back the weakness in my knees. The urethra is the small opening in the top of your penis where urine and semen are released. This kink can include inserting thin metal rods into that tiny hole. You can buy complete sets that include increasingly wider rods for around fifty dollars.

At this point, you might need to take a deep breath. Hang in there. At the very least, I can offer a silver lining for the dick-and-ball-tattoo story. Let's return to the scene. At face value, I did not see any signs of criminality. Medics later reported that the male admitted to using heroin to dull the pain. Although I would never condone the use of this drug, I'd gladly take a painkiller if my boys were under assault. As a result of the call, a subsequent investigation by our drug unit discovered that the tattoo man was selling more than just tattoos. Both he and his girlfriend were later arrested after a confidential informant purchased a large quantity of heroin from them. The bottom line of this story: tattooing the balls ultimately led to prison walls.

CHAPTER FOUR

BESTIALITY

There are few things stranger or more repulsive than bestiality. I say "few" only because this book covers the gamut of offensive activities. The American Psychological Association defines bestiality as "sexual excitement or gratification obtained by a human through anal or genital intercourse or other sexual contact with a nonhuman animal."[19] Frederick the Great, the king of Prussia in the 1700s, was originally thought to have coined the phrase "man's best friend." He was referring to the long history of loyalty and companionship dogs share with humans. If we think back to Alaska's dog diddler earlier in this book, we can see that somewhere along the line, the spirit of this expression got twisted. Surely, this behavior isn't common in a civilized society . . . or is it? Unfortunately, with contemporary websites, books, podcasts, and bestiality parties promoting this practice, it appears to be on the rise.

---

[19] *Bestiality*, (American Psychological Association Dictionary of Psychology, 2023). https://dictionary.apa.org/bestiality.

There are not many academic studies regarding the prevalence of this behavior. One conducted in 1974 by psychologist Morton M. Hunt put participation in this sickening perversion at 4.9 percent for men and 1.9 percent for women.[20] Using the recent U.S. census figures of 2020, that would add up to nearly sixteen million males and over six million females. While those numbers are staggering to think about, other studies confirm that they are in the ballpark. The largest meta-study on bestiality included data spanning between 1948 and 2023. It involved 17,682 participants and found the following key statistics: 4.75 percent of the population engaged in this behavior, with 85 percent of the offenders being male.[21]

From a law enforcement perspective, it's hard to determine how widespread the practice actually is. One thing we do know: bestiality arrests have increased by more than 3,000 percent in the last twenty years. This is despite the fact that the crimes are difficult to discover and rarely disclosed. Those who indulge understandably conceal their activities, knowing the social ramifications if exposed. They seek out like-minded individuals in judgment-free spaces to chat online and share tricks of the trade. Sites such as BeastForum, AnimalFlix, Barnlove, and Petsex have had millions upon millions of registered members. While these forums constantly change their names and websites, they never disappear for long. Animal lovers beware—it's about to get painfully ugly in this chapter.

---

[20] Morton M. Hunt, *Sexual Behavior in the 1970s*, (Chicago: Playboy Press, 1974), 354.
[21] Bedbible Research Center, *How Common Is Bestiality and Zoophilia? Definitions, Facts, and Statistics*, (Bedbible, 2023). https://bedbible.com/how-common-is-bestiality-and-zoophillia-statistics/. Article also viewable at: dougfifer.com.

Fowl Play . . .

If it looks like a duck, walks like a duck, and quacks like a duck, then it probably is a duck. While this normally holds true in everyday life, the outliers often appear in police work, where what you see isn't always what you get. The following story will be an unforgettable case in point.

The Miami-Dade Police Department is the largest law enforcement agency in the southeastern United States and the eighth largest in the country. They are one of the foremost training agencies in the nation and have high academic and social prestige in law enforcement generally. Their influence reaches far and wide; Miami-Dade has instructed officers from every U.S. state as well as over forty-six foreign countries. They rightfully boast on their website, "Our cutting-edge courses not only provide outstanding classroom instruction, but the latest in hands-on exercises to ensure that all aspects have a real-life scenario-based approach." Miami-Dade is considered the Ivy League of learning for cops.

When I was selected to attend a specialized training taught by detectives from this premier law enforcement agency, I was both ready and willing. It was a big-league invite to their coveted homicide investigations course, the *crème de la crème* of police work instruction. I prepped for this subject matter like it was my first day in the police academy, researching any investigative techniques even remotely associated with solving murders. I wanted to show Miami-Dade that Alaska had some smart cookies for cops as well.

It was Monday morning, and I arrived eager for the first day of class. Two investigators with the homicide bureau introduced themselves and reminded us of the heavy workload ahead. They were well groomed, tan, and wearing custom-tailored suits. I was taken aback a bit since "dressing up" in Alaska consists of wearing a Carhartt jacket and new pair of jeans. Surprisingly, these boys had a mafioso look to them, which was a bit intimidating, to put it mildly. We were promptly provided with the course reading materials, including several lengthy case studies of the most brutal murders in our country's history. They told us to commit these cases to memory and prepare for an onslaught of questions regarding what could have been done better. We were informed that our efforts toward this were nonnegotiable; if we didn't like it, we could leave. This all came within the first fifteen minutes, and I wondered what I had gotten myself into. Maybe I had bitten off more than I could chew.

Before the class had time to react to the investigators' lack of pleasantries, it was time to get cracking on our first case. The detectives showed a picture of an autopsy table. The next photo featured a mostly white mallard duck on the autopsy table. The duck appeared deceased, given its contorted body. The third image showed a scalpel, anoscope, tissue forceps, dressing scissors, and swabs. We didn't get a fourth photo; instead, we got the questions "What happened and whodunit?" With everyone dumbfounded, the *Miami Vice*–looking duo stood in front of the class in their dapper suits accompanied by smug smiles and said, "Figure it out." The only thing I was figuring out at this point was that solving homicides might be a little over my head.

You could hear a pin drop as we all quietly tried to make sense of what they were asking. But the deafening silence didn't last long. The instructors soon started calling out individuals for answers. I slid down into my seat and did my best to avoid direct eye contact. I could hear classmate after classmate repeat the phrases "I don't know," "I need more information," and "No clue here." Shaking their heads in disbelief, the instructors continued calling on each one of us. It was obvious that they had a god complex when it came to murder investigations. Several students tried to offer possible scenarios before being quickly shut down with a single word: "Wrong!" Unable to hide, it was finally my turn to answer. Although a long shot, I reasoned the dead duck could be forensic evidence. Similar to animal hair being used to link suspects to a crime scene, I theorized a duck feather might do the same. DNA from the duck must have been the smoking gun that solved a person's murder. While I anxiously awaited my beatdown for being off target, one of the detectives perked up and asked my name. *My, oh, my*, I thought, *have I hit pay dirt and gotten it right?* With a bit of self-confidence back, I told him, "I go by Fifer." He smiled widely and replied, "Well, Fifer, you're wrong."

At this point, I had had just about enough. These guys were arrogant assholes and seemed to take pleasure in mocking the entire class. I was already miserable an hour into the training, with no end in sight. Cops usually have thick skins, but these guys were getting under it, for sure. Maybe Miami-Dade wasn't all that it was cracked up to be. One detective asked if anyone had anything intelligent to offer. I was thinking it might help if they spent less time tanning and more time refining their people skills, but I held my tongue. With the class stumped and speechless, our instructors didn't hold back: "Solving homicides isn't for the weak-minded. We were hoping to see some real talent come through, and unfortunately, you have let us down." I was getting more and more irritated by the minute. What did they reasonably expect us to solve by looking at three photographs with no additional background information? We weren't the idiots; these guys were the idiots.

Just as I was summoning up the courage to push back, one detective announced it was obvious the class was intimidated by true greatness. He suggested we take a break and consider how fortunate we were to have them as instructors. As the class collectively cringed, he quickly followed up: "But before we do, I have one last thing to say: we're just fucking with you." I'll be damned! They played the role of intimidating cops, acting gruff and arrogant only to mess with us. We had swallowed their fake pompous behavior hook, line, and sinker. The joke was certainly on us, but were the duck photos also a ruse? On the contrary, they were in fact the real deal, which turned into one hell of an icebreaker as a welcome to the class. All playing now aside, the actual chain of events which led to the duck's demise will most certainly ruffle some feathers.

It all started with a little old lady who lived across from a city park located in a small suburban town in southern Florida. The neighborhood was upscale and consisted mostly of older retirees. A large pond was in the park, surrounded by perfectly manicured grass and tall palm trees. This was a favorite hangout for locals and wildlife alike, a perfect setting to relax and enjoy nature. The water attracted many species of birds, but ducks were the predominant visitor to the pond. The little old lady—we'll call her "Belva"—was quite fond of the animals in the park. Swans, squirrels, ducks, iguanas—it didn't matter to her. Belva loved watching them all. As we all know, the older you get, the more important rules become. Senior citizens like to follow routines and rules. Think of your grandparents, up at 5:00 a.m., dinner at 3:00 p.m., in bed by 7:00 p.m. If the speed limit says fifty-five miles per hour, they'll round down to thirty miles per hour to avoid any possible chance of going over. Don't get me wrong—these golden agers are rock-solid citizens who deserve our respect.

With regard to Belva, she epitomizes this wonderful generation. Despite standing at five feet, four inches, and weighing 120 pounds, she didn't put up with any lawbreakers. Far from it—Belva would rain terror down on any potential violators. She considered herself the "park police" and made sure people respected Mother Nature. In particular, she had a few pet peeves when it came to visitors not abiding by the posted rules. Picking up after your dog was one of them. Belva would openly scold the pooch's owner until they grabbed a doggy bag and cleaned up the mess. The park was also a designated quiet zone, so playing loud music was another no-no. Belva would remind visitors to turn off their ungodly noise. If it wasn't Frank Sinatra singing, she wouldn't even call it music. And if park guests ignored the feisty senior, she had a secret weapon: Belva had the local police department on speed dial and would not hesitate to make the call. Most people would simply give up at this point, comply with her demands, and obey the rules.

Belva's most serious perception of injustice was when park-goers fed the ducks, and this was by far the most frequent misdeed, as everyone enjoyed feeding the waterfowl. Several signs were posted around the pond clearly stating, "Please do not feed the ducks." This became Belva's passion after she watched a news story about the harmful effects of giving ducks bread. High-carb diets can cause the birds to become malnourished and defecate more. The increased duck poop can spread disease and upset the ecosystem. Worse yet, baby ducklings do not develop properly and often die when fed a consistent diet of bread. In the end, feeding also leads to waterfowl becoming habituated to humans, which contributes to an increased risk of being vulnerable to predation. This was game, set, and match for Belva; she was now an animal rights activist for ducks.

Time and time again, she scolded park patron after park patron for feeding the wildlife. Belva typically included a lecture as to why this behavior was harmful. It didn't matter if it was a single person or a family with kids—they all got the same message. It was a constant battle for her to enforce this rule, but luckily for the ducks, Ms. Belva was in it to win it. Despite being in her mid-eighties, Belva's mind was as sharp as a steel trap. She would remember if she'd caught you feeding the ducks before, so if she saw you again, it was double trouble for you this time around. Belva would ask for your name or write down your vehicle plate number. She'd then call the local police precinct and report the wrongdoing. The neighborhood cops knew her well after all of this. They'd offer Belva a smile, take the information, and let her know they were on the case. This was merely meant to appease her, as no additional investigation took place. Little kids and parents feeding ducks do not elevate them to the FBI's most wanted list of criminals.

Belva kept a notebook with times and dates of violations for park visitors she deemed repeat offenders. If they arrived in a vehicle, she recorded the make, model, and license plate. One guy whom she called a "frequent flier" would regularly show up and feed the ducks. He would bring multiple loaves of bread and blatantly disregard the rules. Belva talked with the man, who repeatedly ignored her pleas to stop harming the wildlife. Frustrated, she even shared the recent news story she'd watched on why the behavior was so damaging. The man was unfazed and continued tearing and tossing small pieces of bread. Unbeknownst to the bird feeder, he had quickly become public enemy number one in Belva's eyes. And in accordance with her standard protocol, she reported each incident to the police.

The man kept coming to the park, and Belva kept a watchful eye on him. By this time, the ducks were so used to the constant feedings that they were taking bread from his open hand. This was the last straw for Belva; something had to be done. Figuring the police had already read this gentleman the Riot Act, she decided to reach further and call the Florida Fish and Wildlife Conservation Commission, the Department of Elder Affairs, and several state politicians for help. She was given a polite brush-off each time. Her trusting nature assumed the mighty wheels of government were turning and the duck feeder's days were numbered. To help these agencies, Belva continued taking notes on arrival and departure times.

The rule breaker drove the same small blue sedan with Florida plates. Belva's front window faced the park with a bird's-eye view to the goings-on. The guy's MO was usually a midafternoon visit for about thirty minutes. On one occasion, the man returned to the park for a second time in the same day. It was now early evening, and Belva watched intently as the male once again began feeding the ducks. The park was nearly empty except for a dog walker passing through. She wondered why the duck feeder was back so late in the day. A group of ducks had converged around him, and the man, as usual, started hand feeding them. Outraged, Belva called the police once again. She was told they'd send an officer to drive through the park when one was free.

A few minutes later, she saw something that shocked her. The man grabbed a white duck that was eating bread from his hand. He quickly tucked it under his arm and headed back to his car. He got into the driver's side of the vehicle and shut the door. Thinking that he was about to take off with a stolen duck, Belva dialed 911. The police dispatcher assured her they'd send an officer out. Belva then provided a timeline of recent visits, the male's description, and his car's license plate. This was about the tenth time the department had received the same information, but the call taker remained patient and sympathetic. During the call, the car never moved. It had now been ten minutes since he snatched the duck. While Belva was being assured the police were on their way, the driver's door popped open, and the duck was thrown out. The vehicle then started up and drove away. The duck squirmed on the ground for a bit and then went limp.

This time, the cavalry was coming, although the responding officer was skeptical as to the validity of the situation. After all, Belva was in her eighties, and eyesight tends to diminish as we get older. As he pulled into the park, lo and behold, he saw a dead duck. The officer looked at the bird and moved it slightly with his boot. Without knowing why it was dead, he reported the findings to dispatch and asked that another officer respond to the suspect's residence. Since Belva had already provided the vehicle's plate, officers knew just where to go. It was about a twenty-minute drive from the park and was in the same police jurisdiction. The second officer arrived at the residence shortly thereafter and reported the suspect vehicle was not in the driveway, nor did the property have a garage. Without much else to go on, the officer would have to follow up at a later time.

But just as the patrolman was about to leave, the suspect arrived home and pulled in his driveway. The officer quickly got out of his cruiser and walked up to contact the driver. Unaware of the police presence at first, the male started to open his car door, but as soon as he saw the officer, he completely froze. Remember the news story Belva saw about the many reasons why feeding ducks is a bad idea? One of the key points from this segment was that waterfowl who are fed also tend to become habituated to humans, which leads to increased vulnerability to predation. In this case, truer words were never spoken. The male's crotch area was covered in white duck feathers and blood. His pants were unzipped and still partially pulled down, exposing his genitals.

The officer arrested the male with some interesting instructions: "Slowly step out of the vehicle, do not touch your pants, and place your hands behind your back." I have to give this cop credit; he was thinking about preserving evidence despite it being a sticky situation. The initial officer at the park collected the murdered mallard as evidence. A necropsy was later performed to confirm the cause of death. As it turned out, the earlier photos shown to our class were 100 percent authentic. The anoscope tool had been used to view the lining of the duck's cloaca, Latin for "sewer," which acts as a waste elimination chamber for both urine and feces. This was where penile entry was made. The animal coroner's findings: theriocide (animal homicide) due to internal hemorrhaging from sexually related trauma. This was the official medical description for sodomizing a duck to death. The final nail in the suspect's coffin came when blood samples taken from him were found to be a DNA match to the victimized duck. At the end of the class, we were given a post-course evaluation. The top of the form pledged that Miami-Dade prides itself on ensuring the student experience is second to none. Well, fuck a duck—they succeeded!

Makin' Bacon . . .

Does it get any better than waking up to the smell of sizzling bacon in the morning? That mouthwatering aroma is undeniable for most, but can you love bacon too much? Consider your health before you shout, "Hell to the no!"—it's always wise to keep moderation in mind. I mean, nobody wants weight gain, clogged arteries, or heart disease. Now, don't get me wrong—I love bacon as much as the next person. It's just that some like it a little more—or should we say *a lot* more—than others. I once attended a police training in Seattle where I learned of a rather abnormal use for bacon. I'm not talking about putting bacon bits on ice cream, indulging in bacon-flavored vodka, or eating bacon-wrapped sushi. It's safe to say that what I learned in Seattle won't be found in any recipe book.

A favorite activity of cops who spend time working for other agencies is to share the strangest police calls in their respective areas. It is almost a game of one-upmanship, determining who has the most outlandish story. In almost every instance, the competition quickly turns to something sexually offensive. It's not that murders, hostage negotiations, or armed robberies lack interesting or shareable information. It's more that odd sexual fetishes heighten our curiosity because, as cops, we are more shocked by them due to their unfamiliarity. If your coworker tells you about a minor traffic accident they were involved in, you'd respectfully listen and offer the appropriate sympathy. If that same coworker informed you the boss had unexpectedly masturbated in front of them, your response would obviously be much different. You'd still offer moral support and express outrage, but you'd probably be intrigued and much more interested in the details. Traffic accidents happen every day, but your boss lone-rangering in the office hopefully doesn't.

It's human nature to be intrigued by the unknown, especially anything sexually related. You would remember the boss incident ten years later with surprising clarity, but you likely wouldn't recall one detail of the minor traffic accident. Our brains are undoubtedly hardwired for this behavior. An Ohio State University study showed that men think about sex nineteen times a day, while women think about it ten times per day.[22] That's 6,935 thoughts annually for the fellas and 3,650 for the ladies. We can further solidify our unquenchable thirst for carnal knowledge by looking at Pornhub's 2023 "Year in Review." As one of the largest porn sites, they receive over forty billion yearly visits. That's more than 115 million per day, with the U.S. dominating other countries for the highest traffic. The Philippines, France, Mexico, and the United Kingdom round out the top five. An astounding million-plus hours of new content is added to Pornhub each year, which would take well over one hundred years to watch. Combined with all internet pornography, the numbers become inconceivable. It's not just the guys watching either. Female viewership has been steadily increasing year over year and currently sits at 36%. Not surprisingly, mobile devices now download 91.3% of content viewed.[23]

So, what does bacon have to do with any of this? We all seek sexual pleasure—the numbers don't lie—but what stimulates our sexual cravings can sometimes be at repulsive extremes. In Seattle, as we started the roundtable of competitive cases among our law enforcement counterparts, we quickly found a top

[22] Emily Caldwell, *Study Debunks Stereotype That Men Think About Sex All Day Long,* (Ohio State News, 2011). https://news.osu.edu/study-debunks-stereotype-that-men-think-about-sex-all-day-long/.
[23] https://www.pornhub.com/insights/2023-year-in-review
Articles also viewable at: dougfifer.com.

contender. This officer worked for the city of Fife, Washington. A city founded in 1957, one of Fife's claims to fame is its fertile farmlands. As you'll soon learn, this representation is spot on, although, in this case, in a most unwholesome way. Often in our profession, police officers will work overtime details to make a little extra cash. On this fateful night, "bringing home the bacon" was redefined.

The officer doing overtime was assigned to work an agricultural area that had been riddled with thefts. As you might imagine, stealing farm machinery can be quite lucrative for thieves. While checking parking lots and large barns doesn't seem like much fun, for a cop trying to make ends meet, it certainly helps pay the bills. His shift started off mundanely, without anything of interest. Most properties were private farms that housed a variety of animals and equipment. The parking lots were often full during the day, hosting auctions and public events. At night, they became ghost towns. Typically, you could not have an easier gig driving from empty lot to empty lot. For this cop, however, the night would offer an atypical twist.

As he rechecked a parking area, he noticed a truck he had not seen earlier in the night. It was unoccupied and located in a spot directly in front of several large metal barns. The truck was parked normally and didn't appear staged for a quick getaway. Thieves tend to back in and park close, especially when stealing items such as heavy equipment. The officer thought perhaps he had missed the vehicle previously. It could have been broken down, left by an employee, or parked there for any number of reasons. As any cop would do, he ran a check of the plate, but it yielded nothing—the car was not stolen, and there were no warrants associated with the owner. All appeared quiet in farmland, or so he thought. As a last measure, the officer felt the hood to gauge the temperature. This is a simple cop trick to confirm a vehicle has not been driven recently. The hood can stay warm from engine use for over an hour. To his surprise, it was still very warm.

Somebody was around, and it was his job to find out why. As a safety measure, he called for backup. As soon as the additional officer arrived, they started by checking the closest barn first. It appeared completely dark, and the doors were closed. They entered through a side man door rather than use the over-sized sliding front doors. This offered a little more stealth in their approach. Cops carry extremely bright LED flashlights because entering dark places is not uncommon in their profession. Furthermore, finding light switches in unfamiliar buildings can be difficult and distracting. This barn was about the size of your neighborhood Costco.

Upon entry, it was quickly evident the building was a livestock barn. It did not appear to have any valuable equipment; instead, it housed cows, chickens, goats, horses, and pigs. This was good news for the officers because no theft or burglary also meant no paperwork. Everything was quiet except for the occasional animal noise. As they methodically made their way around the vast number of stalls, they could see a low flickering light toward the back of the barn. At first, this didn't raise much concern. It's not unusual for a building of that size to have some type of inner night lighting. They'd simply check it out and call it a wrap—or so they thought.

We have all had instances where our eyes played tricks on us. A first glance at something might shock us, whereas a second glance reveals we didn't see what we thought we saw. This is perfectly normal, as our brains sometimes process and interpret images incorrectly. It takes approximately one tenth of a second for light entering our pupils to reach our retina and then our brains. This is called a neural lag, or delay. Researchers believe the brain attempts to guess the future based on previous images in that one tenth of a second, sometimes producing misleading results. When the officers found the source of the flickering light, which turned out to be a dim lantern in a stall, they used their flashlights to further investigate. The neural lag provided a mental image of a half-naked man fucking a three-hundred-pound pig doggy style. Unfortunately for the officers, the deceptive one-tenth-of-one-second rule did not apply here. When their eyes caught up to their brain, they were able to confirm that the male was still aggressively going to town.

This is a WTF moment in every cop's career. We are taught to react quickly in situations and take control. A momentary lapse of action is rare, but in this case, quite understandable. What was more astonishing was that the suspect, for lack of better words, did not stop porking the pig when the officers arrived. The male was so thoroughly engrossed in his activity, he was completely oblivious to the two police officers shining their bright flashlights directly onto him. One of the officers finally shouted, "What the hell are you doing?" This resulted in an immediate reaction. The suspect quickly fell back, spun around, and stood up with giant eyes of bewilderment. The dynamic had quickly turned—instead of the officers being temporarily frozen, the perp was now a deer in the headlights. He was described as a heavyset white male in his mid-sixties wearing only a T-shirt.

As the officer in Seattle matter-of-factly continued describing the encounter, he looked at me with a smug smile and said, "That's not the best part." My immediate response: "Get the fuck outta here!" *Let me get this straight*, I thought. *A guy literally playing in pig slop is not the most memorable part?* I was now riveted and couldn't fathom what could top this. He continued with the story, telling me that as they contemplated what to do, they noticed the man was covered in fecal matter from the waist down. His T-shirt, which was white in color, was also partially stained with feces. But it was perhaps the shirt itself that left even a seasoned cop speechless. Printed on the shirt were the words "DIRTY OLD MAN."

As the investigation unfolded, they discovered they had found a serial pig molester. I hate to sound like an infomercial but . . . wait, there's more! The suspect, caught with his pants down, provided bizarre reasons for his bestial liaisons. He admitted to having a sexual fetish for poop. In normal human relationships, he had difficulty finding partners similarly attracted to the sight, scent, and texture of poop. I'm guessing you are now having a WTF moment yourself, but this is common enough that Merriam-Webster has a definition for this fetish:

Coprophilia: marked interest in excrement, especially the use of feces or filth for sexual excitement.

You literally can't make this shit up. Let's circle back to when the officers first encountered the male. At that moment, the suspect continued with his deviant act despite them being right there. It was the overwhelming mess of poop—his *coprophilia*—that excited him. As he anally assaulted the pig, the animal responded by defecating, which only added to the man's sexual gratification. I'm guessing nobody's swiping right on this guy's Tinder feed. As for your likely million-dollar question, "What happened to the pig man? Did they lock him up and throw away the key?" Not exactly—this perverse adventure has one more twist to offer. Unbelievably, humping a hog, prior to 2006, was not illegal in the state of Washington. I'm sure you probably had to reread that last sentence. One might wonder—and quite appropriately—how could this be possible? The answer to that question lies within our next story.

A Stable Relationship . . .

Bestiality was not criminalized in Washington until 2006. Now, before we tongue-lash the Evergreen State, we might take into consideration that the U.S. still has one state that doesn't have a law prohibiting sexual abuse of animals: as of 2024, West Virginia still lacks a law criminalizing bestiality. New Mexico, Wyoming, and Hawaii have only recently enacted regulations banning this reprehensible act. Wyoming's move to outlaw such behavior was prompted by an incident in 2020. A man was caught by a trail camera engaging in sex acts with horses. Police caught the suspect, who admitted to sexual activities with two different fillies. Despite an apparent slam-dunk case, the male could not be prosecuted because there was no statute criminalizing such behavior. Let's look at Hawaii. In 2019, their state legislature passed HB127. If you are thinking this bill outlaws animal sexual abuse, you'd be wrong. Nope—this law fined people $500 for not picking up their pet's poop. Meanwhile, it was still okay to molest animals; it wasn't until late 2021 that bestiality became criminal. To put it mildly, the Aloha State might have their priorities mixed up. Don't get me wrong, I'm all for picking up your dog's droppings, but I'm even more strongly in favor of sending animal rapists to prison.

An appalling fact is that every state in the U.S. has documented cases relating to bestiality. It's not only a national issue, but because of its global prevalence, countries worldwide are also currently enacting laws to prevent such behavior. While it's hard to sugarcoat bestiality, some attempt to disguise the act's nastiness by using less offensive phraseology. "Zoophilic" means having an attraction to or preference for animals. "Zoosexual" is a sexual orientation toward animals. "Zoophiles" are people who are sexually attracted to animals. These euphemistic terms are derived from the same Latin root, but however you describe a predilection for animals, in the end, a leopard can't change its spots. So how might these birds of a feather flock together?

We need not look any further than the good, the bad, and the ugly of the internet. Prior to the online world's proliferation, zoophilia and bestiality forums were tucked away and out of sight. Once relegated to the dark web, these fetishes can now be accessed using popular search engines like Google. Websites are but a click away, sharing videos and promoting locations as legal destinations for visitors who are looking to have sex with animals. Zoophiles and zoosexuals have community forums online that encourage and describe their intimate interactions with animals.

As if that wasn't sick enough, how about listening to a podcast called "Zooier than Thou," which actively advocates sexual intercourse with animals? It gets worse—these podcasts have been uploaded to YouTube, where anyone can hear them. Several online petitions have attempted to remove this channel, but remarkably, it still exists. Feeling a little nauseous? Wait until you lay eyes on the podcast's advertisement and absurd public statement below. They have the audacity to speak of animal activism and cross-species romance in the same breath:

> *Zooier Than Thou is the world's first monthly podcast covering the zoophile community and all things zooey and wonderful. Featuring in-depth discussions, dating advice, and original songs and skits, all with a great deal of playful candor, Zooier Than Thou sets itself apart with an openly positive and joyful interpretation of what it is to be a zoophile.*

> *Over the years, ZooTT has grown to include a multitude of hosts and guests, collectively bringing decades of animal activism and cross-species romance to the mic, with the help of a dedicated cast and crew of zooey talent. There may be others out there doing the same thing, but ZooTT aims to do it the best![24]*

And just when you thought this conduct was not capable of becoming any more irrational, zoophiles have the audacity to mock those who engage in the act of bestiality, somehow distinguishing this from their own zoophilic activity. On this peculiar moral high ground, they consider bestiality an act of nonconsensual sex with an animal, while zoophilia is regarded as consensual sex, permitted by both "partners." I may be going out on a limb here, but if you are mating with nonhuman animals, it's automatically nonconsensual!

By this point, we have learned way too much about the depravity existing within humanity. But let's get back to our

---

[24] "Zooier Than Thou," https://zoo.wtf/.

prior pig molester, "Dirty Old Man," and discover how he was able to avoid prosecution. Sadly—and it bears repeating—having sex with animals was not punishable by law prior to 2006 in the state of Washington. It's hard to fathom how these laws throughout the country have taken so long to be enacted and inconceivable that anyone would oppose their passing. But in Washington, it would take a stomach-churning turn of events in 2005 that would ultimately force the state to do what was right. Unfortunately, as is all too common, a death had to occur before legislators acted. Spoiler alert: this time, it wouldn't be the defenseless animal who bought the farm.

It started with a zoophile who distributed animal porn under the alias of "Mr. Hands." This was, in fact, Kenneth Pinyan, an unassuming man whose activity sums up the back cover synopsis of this book perfectly. He is why "you'll never look at your neighbor the same way," why "you'll wonder about your best friend," and why "you'll imagine what your coworker does behind closed doors." You see, we could drop Kenneth Pinyan in Anytown, U.S.A. He exists everywhere, whether you want to believe it or not.

Pinyan was a Boeing engineer, who, by all appearances, was well educated and successful. He was previously married, had children, and lived in Old Harbor, Washington. His friends, family, and neighbors had little insight into his Jekyll-and-Hyde personality. Those of us who work nine-to-five jobs understandably relish their weekend fun. We might be excited to catch a movie, host a barbecue, or book a tee time. Mr. Hands, meanwhile, looked forward to fucking horses on his weekends, specifically one stud referred to as "Big Dick." As jarring and unpleasant as this sexual fixation may seem to us, it leads to an even more implausible series of events that took place in Enumclaw, Washington.

This quaint little town of about twelve thousand residents is less than an hour drive from Seattle. The land on which Enumclaw sits, often called the "Plateau," was formed by volcanic mudflow that spewed from Mount Rainier nearly six thousand years ago. According to legend, Native Americans who lived in the area feared the continual volcanic activity. The loud and frightening crashing sounds from inside the mountain would lead to its name. Enumclaw, in the native Salish (prounounced "SAY-lish") language means "home of evil spirits." As it turned out, this was one hell of a premonition because in 2005, this pint-size city would have a media eruption unlike any they'd seen before.

The Enumclaw horse sex case took place on the fateful day of July 2. Someone anonymously dropped off an ailing Pinyan at the local community hospital, pleading for medical treatment for his friend. The unidentified male made a quick exit before medical staff discovered that Pinyan had died in the emergency waiting room. At the age of forty-five, Mr. Hands's farewell performance would thrust into the spotlight a subject matter people did not want to think about. A subsequent investigation by the King County Sheriff's Department would leave investigators stunned. Fortunately for them, a hospital surveillance camera captured the license plate of the vehicle Pinyan had arrived in. With that information, detectives were, quite literally, off to the races. A nearby farm was searched, and authorities seized hundreds of hours of videotapes depicting unfathomable sexual acts upon animals. The video depicting the act that resulted in Kenneth Pinyan's death was among those collected.

This case was one of the catalysts for animal rights groups to start fighting back. In fact, anti-zoophile organizations are turning to social media to combat the dramatic increase in this behavior. For example, a community statement and informational video description from the Anti-Zoophilia Society reads partly as follows:

> The whole idea of this account is to educate and inform other people of the dangers of sexual crimes against animals [sic] are not exceptional, isolated incidents. The case facts run a wide range from individual animals assaulted by their owners in their homes, to organized bestiality events held in clandestine, often rural locations.[25]

The Humane Society of the United States actively supports legislation prohibiting bestiality. They also honor law enforcement and prosecutors who put offenders behind bars. Stop Animal Sexual Assault (SASA) is a nonprofit organization devoted to increasing public awareness of animal sexual assault, and they promote the increase in severity of penalties for violations. They justly seek to make animal rape illegal in all states and territories of the U.S. SASA unmasks these real-world predators on their website as well as provides a bestiality map showing where and what types of animals were assaulted. One of the largest studies of bestiality-related arrests was published in 2019. It showed dogs were the most frequent victims, followed by horses and a host of farm animals such as cattle, goats, chickens, and pigs.

---

[25] "Anti-Zoophilia," YouTube account, accessed April 4, 2024, https://www.youtube.com/user/AntiZoophilia.

Other species made this list as well: reptiles, wildlife, cats, and birds. In 72.5 percent of these cases, animal victims lived with or were known to the offender.[26]

As disturbing as this is, the nightmare won't soon be over for any of us because this true story about Mr. Hands getting fucked by a stallion called "Big Dick" will haunt your mind forever. It's hard to grasp that Kenneth Pinyan enjoyed being filmed while having sex with horses. In order to tell this story accurately, we have to be more specific: he was the taker, never the giver. But how did he get the studhorses to mate with him? He would strip down, cover himself with horse-breeding pheromones, and bend over. Mr. Hands was a bottom boy until the end.

The medical examiner's office would rule his death accidental, describing the cause as acute peritonitis due to perforation of the colon. Video evidence would show Pinyan wasn't alone in committing these acts. A group of men would meet up, film themselves being sodomized by horses, then upload the videos. They called themselves "zoos," and many of these recordings are still available online. The subsequent community outcry and media response would cause legislators to pass Senate Bill 6417 on February 11, 2006, banning bestiality in Washington State and making acts of this nature a felony.

But unlike Mr. Hands, the story didn't die there. A documentary of the life and death of Kenneth Pinyan debuted at the Sundance Film Festival in 2007. Titled *Zoo*, it received multiple

---

[26] M. Jenny Edwards, *Arrest and Prosecution of Animal Sex Abuse (Bestiality) Offenders in the United States, 1975-2015,* (The Journal of the American Academy of Psychiatry and the Law, 2019). https://jaapl.org/content/early/2019/05/16/JAAPL.003836-19#:~:text=Animal victims most often lived,) (n = 17). Article also viewable at: dougfifer.com.

independent film awards. I'm not sure which is creepier—the story or the movie poster.

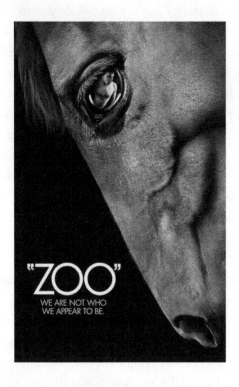

People's fascination with this case has stood the test of time. *The Joe Rogan Experience* podcast has talked about Mr. Hands on multiple episodes. And although we don't want to accept that these types of horrific acts can occur, we also can't seem to get enough.

Dead Meat . . .

While the previous stories of duck defiling, pig penetration, and lusting for horse cock are downright shocking, Alaska has its own special flavor of animal taboo. This next case involves the horrible act of necrobestiality. You can probably figure it out based on the word itself, but I'll translate anyway: it's having sex with dead animals. To get us started, let me introduce you to one of Alaska's largest and most dangerous animals. No, not the 1,500-pound Kodiak brown bear, though that's a great guess. We'll actually be talking about moose. These big boys can weigh upwards of 1,600 pounds and top out at nearly seven feet. Nowhere else in the world do they grow larger, and Alaska has around two hundred thousand roaming free. With a resident human population of roughly seven hundred thousand, this equals one moose for every three to four people. These crowded numbers show why more people in Alaska are injured by moose than bears each year. In practical terms, if a brown bear grabs ahold of you, it's game over, but there are only around thirty thousand of them in Alaska, so the chances of encountering them are far lower.

If you are cringing at the thought of what comes next, yes, a moose corpse is about to get violated. I get it—most people inherently have a natural love for animals. I'm a huge dog lover; our family pooch is named Malbec, and she means the world to me. If police work has taught me one thing, it's that people's repellent behaviors make me love my dog even more, and I'm sure most of you can relate. Studies prove this, as well, showing we have higher levels of empathy for our pets than our adult counterparts. I have seen this in action while investigating a tragic vehicle accident. The driver in one car died on impact whereas the other vehicle's occupants survived, except for their dog. The pups' owners were inconsolable at the loss—not for the dead driver, just for their family pet. I'm okay with crying for our four-legged friends, but in fairness, the other guy deserved a few tears too, even if he wasn't part of their family. (If you were wondering about Malbec's name, all our pets are named after grapes, which points to our family's condition of "novinophobia"—the fear of running out of wine. At least we don't have a "necro-" prefixing our passion).

There is no easy way to tell this story, so I am just going to rip off the Band-Aid. A moose had died for unknown reasons near a heavily used trail along the coast of Anchorage. The body was off in the woods a bit, and passersby were concerned because they had seen a man loitering around the area recently. Over the next several days, the man started to build a makeshift wall concealing the moose. Locals were worried he was illegally harvesting the meat. Since Alaska has a high number of moose deaths, a state program exists to salvage whatever is left. Typically, this involves incidents of roadkill, which is how six hundred to eight hundred of these animals are killed each year. Remarkably, that amounts to around 250,000 pounds of organic free-range meat now up for grabs. And roasted moose meat is quite delicious and an excellent source of vitamins and minerals. It's also extremely low fat and a much better dietary choice than beef. Moose is such a delicacy that citizens will start carving off steaks from the carcass if they happen upon one of these fallen giants. To prevent this from happening unsafely, the state requires residents to be on a qualified list of meat harvesters—if you're not on the list, no free moose steaks for you.

Cops were called in to check out the suspicious loiterer in Anchorage. It was a hot summer day by Alaska standards—seventy degrees Fahrenheit—so a pleasurable walk with epic scenery didn't seem too bad to the officers. That changed quickly when they found the dead moose's location. It was just as reported: a small wall had been built about fifty feet off the trail. The wall had been built with driftwood, branches, sticks, and leaves. At first, they couldn't see the moose or anyone else, but the distinct, foul odor of death was present. If you've never caught a whiff of death, I can't emphasize this enough: the stench is unmistakable. The officers initially thought a call to the Alaska Department of Fish and Game would take care of the problem. Dead moose attract bears, who then aggressively protect their food sources. This poses an extreme danger in densely populated areas such as Anchorage, so the carcass is quickly removed. One of the officers made his way to the wall to have a look at the moose. He needed to know how big it was for transportation purposes because moose often require a tow truck with a strong winch due to their immense size.

That's when things got weird. As soon as he peered over, a man jumped up while simultaneously pulling up his pants. The moose was on its side with the male suspect standing near the hindquarters. The horror-stricken cop reluctantly asked, "Were you just fucking a dead animal?" The man denied the moose molestation but didn't have any other reason for being there. His pants were covered in moose fur and "purge fluid," which is probably not what you are thinking it is. No, it wasn't the suspect's ejaculate. "Purge fluid" is merely the decomposition juice that leaks out of a carcass's oral and nasal passages, as well as other cavities. Did the cops call out the CSI team? For the purpose of a forensic examination, 1,600 pounds of rotting moose meat would be a sloppy mess, so a formal inquiry was unnecessary. When I heard about the call, I asked the officer, "Was he really fucking the moose?" He answered, "He was definitely fucking the moose."

CHAPTER FIVE

NECROPHILIA

E ven though the onslaught of bestiality and necrobestiality was no doubt mentally taxing for you, there's no rest for the wicked here, so we're on to yet another vile act known as necrophilia. It comes from the Greek roots "philia" (meaning attraction or love) and "nekros" (meaning dead body). Put the two together, and we get sexual intercourse with or attraction to corpses. While most of us wouldn't get down and dirty with the dead, this abhorrent behavior is not as uncommon as you might think. In fact, written records indicate it was practiced in ancient Egypt. Embalmers from more than five thousand years ago couldn't seem to keep it in their pants. Fortunately, those who built the mighty pyramids had a solution for this problem. They would leave a deceased woman in the hot sun decaying for several days prior to embalming. Since a dead body itself wasn't a turn off, especially when preserved with embalming, the putrid smell of an untreated corpse did the trick.[27] As crazy as this twisted desire seems, what follows next will bring a new meaning to the expression "dead lay."

While one might think "lust for a corpse" doesn't need any further explanation, this perverted sexual behavior nonetheless has three main subcategories:

1. Necrophilia, fantasy

2. Necrophilia, normal

3. Necrophilia, homicide

Playing Possum . . .

Let's start off with the necrophilia fantasy. It's just as it sounds: using your mind to visualize having sex with a dead body. While men and women both participate in this type of fantasy, research has found nearly 95 percent of necrophiles are male.[28] This behavior isn't unique to any specific state, but as you are probably learning, Alaska's sexual deviates strive for that next level of freakishness. Knowing that Alaska has one of the lowest populations in the country, you might wonder why there are so many sexual outliers among them. It might be the darkness, cold, or remoteness that mentally triggers some of this wickedness. Another, more likely reason is that Alaska is simply a magnet for odd ducks. The Last Frontier prides itself on being wild and free,

---

[27] *Necrophilia in Ancient Egypt*, (Yonder Worlds, 2009). https://yonderworlds.wordpress. com/2017/09/14/necrophilia-in-ancient-egypt-herodotus-isis-osiris-seth-mythology/. Article also viewable at: dougfifer.com.

[28] Jonathan P. Rosman and Phillip J. Resnick, *Sexual Attraction to Corpses: A Psychiatric Review of Necrophilia*, (The Bulletin of the American Academy of Psychiatry and the Law 17, no. 2, 1989), 156. https://jaapl.org/content/jaapl/17/2/153.full.pdf. Article also viewable at: dougfifer.com.

and for those who don't quite fit in elsewhere, this sounds like the opportune place to be.

Now you might take this in the wrong way at first, but over time, cops become friendly with prostitutes. No, this doesn't mean we're buying what they're selling. What it means is that we get access to their street knowledge. Because of their lifestyle, they know far more about the community than anyone else. As a beat cop, I would regularly stop and chat with the ladies of the night. This small talk would lay the trusting groundwork for more serious topics at a later date. Did it pay off? Not only did it pay off, but it was the most productive investigative tool I ever used. From theft cases to homicides and everything in between, prostitutes always had the lowdown.

Hooker stories would teach me about those who fantasize about necrophilia. Although not technically a crime, we might want to lock them up anyway, just to be safe. With my sex work acquaintances, I'd always start the small talk with a few basic check-in questions: "How are things going?" "Are you keeping yourself safe?" "Anything new going on?" One girl's answer never changed: "Same shit, different day." She then asked, "Are you married?" I thought her question was a little odd, but in the spirit of mutual respect, I answered, "Yes." She followed up by saying, "Married men are really fucked up, and I feel sorry for their wives." I jokingly responded, "Well, hopefully my wife likes me." That's when I got the story about a john who had a rather unusual role-playing request. It wasn't one of the more typical pay-to-play scenarios such as oral, anal, or bondage. This one had a much darker side to it: he asked her to play dead while he fucked her.

At the time, a normal trick would set you back about fifty bucks. If you asked for something unusual or disturbing, the price went up. She told me she didn't want to play dead for this guy—it creeped her out—so she threw out a number he'd likely turn down. Not only did he accept, but he also became a regular. This john—who I'll simply call "John"—was very specific in his instructions. The sex would usually take place in a hotel, though the location would eventually change. She would lay in the bed, fully clothed, and play dead. John would undress her very slowly and carefully. Prior to having sex, he would masturbate for a few minutes while staring intently at her naked and motionless body. If she moved at all or opened her eyes, he would become upset. She learned John was married, had kids, and was a respected businessman in the community. Later on, he would eventually ask her to come to his house. John's wife and kids were away on a trip to see relatives. Reluctantly, and against her better judgment, she agreed.

John lived in what she called a rich house in a rich neighborhood. He pulled into the garage so his neighbors wouldn't suspect anything, and the two of them went inside. This is when things got far more bizarre. I know what you're thinking, but keep the following in mind: perspective is largely based on a person's circumstances. John's reason for having a prostitute there was because his wife was not into playing dead. She had even mocked him for being messed up in the head when the subject arose. John's twisted revenge for her mockery was to play out his fantasy with a prostitute in the couple's bed. And for a dear price, he got what he wanted. While in the act, John asked that she not breathe so heavily. He could see her chest moving up and down, and it was throwing him off. (If you were against my earlier suggestion to just lock them up, how are you feeling now?) In the end, and oddly enough, a sense of morality would put a stop to this business relationship. But it wasn't Johnny-boy's conscience that kicked in; it was the prostitute's. She didn't like him disrespecting his family on their home turf. Incidentally, if you're wondering how much the necro-sex cost, it was $150 a shot.

Cracking Open a Cold One . . .

Whether it's at a summer barbecue, sporting event, or just a hangout, chilling with the boys, having an ice-cold beer is an all-American tradition. According to the U.S. beer industry, in 2021, brewers sold over 200 million barrels. If we translate that into twenty-four twelve-ounce containers, it's a staggering 2.9 billion cases.[29] That's cracking open a lot of cold ones! Beer is also the alcoholic beverage of choice, according to a recent Gallup poll.[30] The results were: 37 percent beer, 31 percent prefer liquor, 29 percent favor wine, and 3 percent "other." Not surprisingly, men drink it around twice as much as the ladies, with the ladies generally preferring wine over beer. Guys, women might be onto something, and here's why men should prefer wine too: an Italian study, published in *The Journal of Sexual Medicine*, showed red wine increases the sexual appetite of women.[31] While this research is not conclusive by any means, a bit of wine might equal extra sack time.

Are you ready for a truly repulsive and disgusting story about beer? Well, sorry to disappoint, but this isn't really about the brewski. And sorry, ladies, there are no fermented grapes here

[29] *Industry Fast Facts*, (National Beer Wholesalers Association, 2023). https://nbwa.org/resources/fast-fact.

[30] Megan Brenan, *More Than Six in 10 Americans Drink Alcohol*, (*Gallup*, 2023). https://news.gallup.com/poll/509501/six-americans-drink-alcohol.aspx.

[31] Nicola Mondaini, et al, *Regular Moderate Intake of Red Wine Is Linked to a Better Women's Sexual Health*, (The Journal of Sexual Medicine 6, no. 10, 2009). https://pubmed.ncbi.nlm.nih.gov/19627470/. Articles also viewable at: dougfifer.com.

either. Having said that, it is all about rancid and sickening behavior. Fair warning—you might want to grab a stiff drink before we delve into a sexual perversion that will send chills down your spine. Better yet, make it a double—though I wouldn't recommend cracking open a cold one.

Returning to our necrophilic subcategories, next up, we have normal necrophilia. How could anyone doing this fit into a "normal" category? This describes individuals who perform various sex acts with corpses. They don't just fantasize; they actually do the deed. How does one find a body, you might ask? Criminal arrests relating to this behavior suggest regular necrophiles seek employment in specific areas, like mortuaries, funeral homes, hospitals, or cemeteries. Kenneth Douglas, a former coroner's technician in Ohio, admitted to having sex with up to one hundred bodies. He was eventually caught in a rather unusual turn of events. Douglas had sex with a nearly decapitated eighteen-year-old murder victim who was awaiting autopsy. Her killer, a door-to-door salesman named David Steffen, admitted to brutally beating, slashing, and stabbing the victim to death; he also stated that he had wanted to rape her but couldn't get an erection. When investigators told him semen had been found inside the victim, Steffen adamantly denied it was his. A jury didn't believe him and convicted the killer of murder and rape. DNA evidence, however, would later link Douglas as the rapist. I'm not sure which is more remarkable—Douglas hitting the one hundred mark, or the real killer being truthful.[32]

---

[32] The following video includes an audio clip of Douglas talking about his crimes: https://www.youtube.com/watch?v=E1qejygVZSs Video also viewable at: dougfifer.com.

No Glove, No Love . . .

Let's return to the frozen North for yet another shocking case. The medical examiner (ME) system has been active in the U.S. dating back to the 1800s. It's common for people to interchangeably use the terms "coroner" and "medical examiner," but they are not the same. Medical examiners are required to be a physician and become certified by an organization such as the American Board of Pathology. This process can take upwards of twelve years to complete. On the other hand, as improbable as it sounds, nearly anyone can become a coroner, with more than 80 percent being elected with little to no medical background. While the job requirements vary from state to state, the basic standards are minimal: registered voter, eighteen or older, no felony convictions, and a mandatory training program, if elected.

The coroner profession was first established in Great Britain in 1164, and even though the medical examiner should be the modern replacement of that archaic practice, more than 1,500 U.S. counties still operate under the coroner system, according to the National Association of Medical Examiners. From a law enforcement perspective, this is unconscionable. I know how difficult it is to solve homicides even with the best trained forensic pathologist at your side, let alone a Joe-Blow coroner determining the cause of death. While I don't intend to disrespect the responsible members of this profession, it is difficult to trust the varying standards that currently exist for the job. The election and appointment of coroners is outdated and should be abolished.

The FBI reports that national homicides averaged around twenty-two thousand per year so far in the 2020s. This number is undoubtably higher if we consider the lack of professional training afforded most coroners. The five classifications of deaths are natural, undetermined, accidental, suicide, and homicide. At first glance, the determination of these kinds of death seems like a no-brainer, but in real life, it takes a lot of brain power. Apparent suicide can sometimes turn out to be a homicide, while a seemingly "natural" death can also wind up a murder. "Accidental" can become "intentional," and an undetermined death can end up being foul play. The truth depends on having the best of the best investigate murders, and as a civil society, we should expect nothing less.

I have a tremendous amount of experience working with medical examiners and attending autopsies. As mentioned earlier in this book, I worked on a specialized unit (the crime scene response team) that responded to homicides and suspicious deaths. We were the first line of defense in determining if something was either on the up and up or more sinister in nature. The training required for this team was substantial and continuous; it was not an elected position. After several years on the unit, I became proficient in identifying cause and effect and could reconstruct the last minutes of someone's life. I worked with death so much, it reminds me of the famous line in *The Sixth Sense*: "I see dead people." To this day, I can visualize every homicide victim, and not by choice—I still see dead people.

In Alaska, as described on the government website, "the State Medical Examiner Office is responsible for conducting the medical/legal investigative work related to unanticipated, sudden or violent deaths. This includes determining cause and manner of death and providing consultation to law enforcement and the courts."[33] I have always been impressed with the competence dis-

---

[33] *State Medical Examiner Office*, (Alaska Department of Health, 2024). https://health.alaska.gov/dph/medicalexaminer/pages/default.aspx.

played by this office. They work hand in hand with the Anchorage Police Department and are crucial to our investigations. Attending autopsies at the ME's office was one part of my specialized duties. Why would a cop be required to attend autopsies? It's a chain of custody issue; we document and collect any evidence of a suspected crime. MEs aren't sworn law enforcement, and cops aren't pathologists, but we each have a specific function during a postmortem examination.

Honestly, it's a creepy place to be, and even creepier watching bodies being taken apart and put back together. I remember the first time I saw the ME cut a dead body's scalp and pull the person's entire face away. All I could think about was Hannibal Lecter in *The Silence of the Lambs*. What's more amazing is that when the examination ended, the ME stretched the face back into place, returning it to its normal appearance. A postmortem technician then sewed it up nice and tight, leaving it looking as good as new. The next time you're lamenting your job, visualizing this process should help remind you that it could be much worse.

Since I often worked closely with the autopsy technicians, we would occasionally shoot the shit. Invariably the doctor was late, so we had plenty of time for stories. One of my favorite technicians—we'll call him "Ken"—was a unique individual. I thought cops had a savage sense of humor, but this guy was as cold-blooded as they came. In fairness, he was around death 24-7. Ken loved police stories and wanted to know the latest and greatest missteps involving the general public. He particularly liked hearing about police chases and told me he was a big fan of the TV show *Cops*. And since I like a great story as much as the next guy, I encouraged Ken's eagerness to impress me with his stories. So, you can imagine that my ears perked up when Mr. Death himself said, "Are you ready for this one?"

Ken started off by telling me he'd found a blue latex glove with the fingers cut off wadded up in an otherwise empty wastebasket. The wastebasket was in the cold storage area of the medical examiner's building. This area contains individual body coolers which, chilled to around forty degrees, literally keep the meat fresh. Finding a glove here was in and of itself not a big deal, as hundreds are tossed into the trash weekly. What was strange were the missing fingers. As the fingerless gloves kept turning up night after night in the exact same wastebasket, Ken knew something wasn't right.

Upon closer inspection, Ken saw that each of the disposed gloves had a strange substance inside of them. At first, he thought they might have been used to capture some type of bodily discharge during postmortem movement. While this certainly wasn't standard protocol, it was a possibility. Technicians often assist MEs with prepping the body, taking X-rays, and collecting fingerprints. Staff at this time included a chief medical examiner, an assistant medical examiner, death scene investigators, autopsy technicians, and administration support staff. Since most had access to the body storage area, it wouldn't be easy to pinpoint the culprit.

The first clue was provided by the janitorial crew who came in each night to clean. One of their duties was emptying the wastebaskets throughout the building. Since the gloves were typically found free of other trash, the timing of their appearance, following the janitor's shift, showed that the gloves had been tossed at some point late at night. As a result, this period of time eliminated the possibility that support staff, MEs, or death scene investigators had disposed of the gloves because they were not usually in the building at night. This left only a few autopsy technicians in the mix, but among those, only one primarily worked the night shift. And this individual was odd, according to Ken—very odd.

Without cameras and security key cards at the time, Ken was left with only one option. He decided to go through the tech's personal belongings. When asked about the Fourth Amendment, pertaining to unreasonable searches and seizures, Ken replied, "It was only his backpack." I was somewhat joking, as there's really no such thing as an illegal search by a private citizen. Although a workplace ransacking is unethical and might get you fired or sued, it's not a criminal issue. Besides, I wanted to know what the guy had too. When Ken said, "He had multiple bottles of personal lubrication," the darkness of humanity immediately filled my mind. My next question was obvious: "Was he fucking the dead bodies?"

Ken quickly said, "No, nothing that bad. I mean, I don't think he was." For the moment, I was temporarily relieved. I had mentally convicted this poor guy of sex with corpses when he was probably just making workplace whoopee with his girlfriend. In my career, I've caught couples having thrill sex in various places. Whether it's in cemeteries, shopping centers, or office buildings, if there's one thing I've learned, nothing is off limits when it comes to sex. In most cases, having sex in unconventional places involves the excitement of getting caught, the rush of being naughty, and the desire to spice things up. The only problem here was that there wasn't a girlfriend involved, or, for that matter, any living partner. When asked what the guy was doing, Ken answered, "He was masturbating at work nightly."

I started laughing, all the buildup simply for a coworker rubbing one out seemed overkill. Ken then added, "He was masturbating with the dead." My first thought: *The dead can't masturbate.* My second thought: *What exactly does "with the dead" mean?* It meant he liked to look at the female cadavers and jack off into a latex glove. He'd cut four of the fingers off to create a makeshift condom, leaving the thumb for his penis to ejaculate in. After relieving himself, the glove was tossed into the wastebasket. This led to another obvious question: "How do you *know* he wasn't having sex with the bodies?" Somewhat perplexed, Ken replied, "I guess I don't, but he only admitted to masturbating." Now, since he's not a cop, I'll give him a pass on his poor interrogation techniques. I have found that criminals nearly always minimize their transgressions; it's just what they do.

The masturbating autopsy technician also admitted to having a serious drug addiction coupled with family problems, which he claimed had contributed to his misconduct. Ken believed he would not have offered up this additional personal information if he wasn't being truthful. While I wasn't buying it, it's true that the guy did, to some extent, let it all hang out. This case had occurred well before my autopsy days, and the self-pleasuring tech was long gone from the medical examiner's office. But even if I had uncovered this activity, it wouldn't matter from a criminal standpoint because Alaska statutes do not currently prohibit this behavior.

According to AS 11.61.130, "a person commits the crime of misconduct involving a corpse if, except as authorized by law or in an emergency, the person intentionally disinters, removes, conceals, or mutilates a corpse; the person engages in sexual penetration of a corpse; or the person detains a corpse for a debt or demand or upon a lien or charge. Misconduct involving a corpse is a class A misdemeanor." As insane as it sounds, beating off to bodies doesn't even get you a slap on the wrist; you must engage in sexual penetration of a corpse to be charged. To top it off, even if he is caught dead to rights, the culprit only faces a misdemeanor.

After hearing this perverse story, I still couldn't wrap my head around one detail: the tech's need to make improvised condoms. Most guys would just grab a tissue and call it good. Not only that, but how does a latex glove turn into a rubber? Ken and I grabbed a box of gloves, and after a bit of trial and error, we figured it out. Using a pair of scissors, it's two simple steps: start cutting from the pinkie side of the glove and trim off the next four fingers, leaving the thumb intact. When I first saw it, I had no doubt rubber man had been hard at work, but with more than just his hand. The appearance of the adapted glove was also truth serum for Ken: shaking his head back and forth, he said, "Jesus Christ, he *was* fucking the bodies." This case was far more morbid than masturbation. While practicing safe sex is important, "no glove, no love" should only apply to the living.

A One-Sided Affair . . .

The expression "It takes two to tango" usually means both parties need to act cooperatively in order to achieve a desired outcome. While this is true for the most part, we've learned here that sex with the dead is an exception to this rule. Undoubtedly, the prior accounts of fantasy necrophilia, normal necrophilia, and necrobestiality are at the extreme end of the spectrum when it comes to sickening behaviors, but it can and does get worse. Although "most extreme necro" isn't a competition, homicidal necrophilia, our final subcategory, definitely tops them all. This is the act of murdering someone to obtain a corpse for sexual pleasure.

How often this occurs is difficult to determine for several reasons. First and foremost, the vast majority of cases involving vaginal and anal trauma, whether pre- or postmortem, are similar in appearance on the autopsy table. On top of that, live sperm can survive for several days in both living and deceased victims, depending on the surrounding conditions. As a result, forensic science does not have a definitive way of establishing if intercourse occurred before or after death. To sum things up: we can put a man on the moon, yet we can't tell if someone copulated with a cadaver or a living person. Killers often admit to killing, but the stigma of diddling the dead can be too much to bear even for these cold-blooded sadists. In most cases, it takes an admission by the perpetrator as to whether or not the primary motivation was postmortem sex or if the sex acts were secondary deviant behaviors.

While the majority of necrophiles share a common need to possess an unresisting partner, killing for that purpose obviously adds to this evilness. Jeffrey Dahmer, one of America's most infamous serial killers, was openly vocal about this preference. He liked to have complete control over the person, and killing them provided that power. Convicted of fifteen murders, Dahmer would also eat portions of his victims. This would sexually arouse him to the point of performing indecent acts on the remaining body parts. Dahmer was not alone in his sadistic behaviors; Gary Ridgeway, the Green River Killer, is perhaps the most prolific necrophiliac serial killer the world has ever known. Convicted of forty-nine murders, Ridgeway in fact said he stopped counting after killing more than seventy-one young women and girls. After dumping their bodies in the forest, he would revisit the victims' corpses for sex. According to Ridgeway, he only returned to the body for the first few days following the murder—the reason being that he didn't like it when too many flies came around.

Does the act of necrophilia have a connection to serial killers? Although you might not guess, Alaska has the highest rate of serial murderers in the country proportional to its population. It turns out that one of the most beautiful places on Earth is also one of the deadliest. Amongst these killers is Israel Keyes, who intimated during his confession that he had performed the act of necrophilia. He did this after a murder in Anchorage in the winter of 2012. The killing in this gut-wrenching case would brutally end the life of an eighteen-year-old victim named Samantha Koenig. The young woman had been abducted at gunpoint at a local coffee kiosk. Surveillance video would capture the chilling abduction, but where Koenig was taken afterward remained unknown. The Anchorage Police Department and FBI would launch a massive search, with every available officer assigned to the investigation. More than two weeks passed without a trace of her whereabouts; it was as if the suspect and victim had vanished into thin air.

With all leads exhausted, the case finally took a bizarre twist. Samantha's boyfriend received a text from her phone that led APD to a ransom note and Polaroid picture of Samantha. A recent edition of the *Anchorage Daily News* was also captured in the photo to establish proof of life. The kidnapper wanted $30,000 placed into Samantha's bank account. From an investigation standpoint, this was highly unusual. While kidnappers often ask for cash, they don't ask that it be deposited in the victim's account. Attempts to trace Samantha's phone proved unsuccessful as it was turned off in between uses.

Five thousand dollars of the requested funds were deposited by the family. The bank agreed to immediately flag any activity and notify law enforcement. Three withdrawals were made over the next several days at various ATMs around Anchorage.

Though other officers and I raced to each reported location, the kidnapper was gone by the time we arrived. ATM video would show the same masked man wearing a hoodie and dark sunglasses at each location. Just when it seemed like it would be a matter of time before we caught him, the trail went surprisingly cold once again. Then, a few weeks later, a second round of withdrawals started, only this time, ATMs had been accessed in Arizona, New Mexico, and Texas. Cameras would capture the suspect's vehicle, a white Ford Focus, and local police were soon on the lookout. Finally, a vigilant Texas highway patrolman spotted the car and pulled it over for a minor traffic infraction, driving three miles per hour over the speed limit. Israel Keyes was the driver and only occupant in the vehicle. Samantha's debit card and cell phone were found with him, signaling an ominous turn in the investigation.

Keyes initially denied knowing anything about Samantha when he was interviewed in Texas. He was extradited back to Alaska and made some unusual requests prior to talking—it was not for a reduced sentence or media presence. He wanted a Snickers Peanut Butter, an Americano, and a nice cigar. After getting what he wanted, coupled with rapport building by the detectives, Keyes unleashed a horrific and detailed account of murder. The audio confession is numbing to listen to. Hearing it, you realize it isn't just Israel Keyes talking; it's the devil himself.

He confessed to planning to rob the coffee kiosk and kidnap the barista. Keyes was not specifically targeting Samantha; it didn't matter to him which girl was working. He remembered her resisting but was able to use zip ties to gain control. He returned home and placed Samantha in a shed on his property, just feet from his house where his girlfriend and daughter were sleeping. The shed contained tape, ropes, garbage bags, and cutting tools.

Although Samantha had no way of knowing at the time, she was never leaving there alive.

Keyes kept a police scanner on to listen for any reports of the abduction. He demanded her cell phone, debit card, and PIN. She provided the number but told him the phone had been left at the coffee shop and her debit card was in her boyfriend's truck. Brazenly, Keyes went back to the kiosk, retrieved the cell phone, and sent her boyfriend a message as if it were Samantha herself. His intention in doing this was to delay police involvement. He texted the boyfriend to say she was going away with friends for a few days. He then went to Samantha's house and grabbed the debit card from her boyfriend's unlocked truck.

After returning home, Keyes sadistically raped and tortured Samantha throughout the night. He then strangled her to death before hiding her body in one of the shed's cabinets. As implausible as it sounds, Keyes left her there and went on a two-week cruise around the Caribbean islands. When he came back to Alaska, he wasn't in any rush to get rid of the body; his sinister intentions were far from finished. It was February, one of Alaska's coldest months, and Samantha's body was frozen solid.

Keyes used a space heater and hairdryer to thaw her out. He admitted to investigators later that he did things to her while she was warm again, inferring necrophilia, and he took satisfaction at the investigators' disgust. Seeing the angst on their faces, he callously laughed and said, "You have your monster." When asked which serial killer he most related to, he said that he saw himself being closest to one of America's most vicious killers, Ted Bundy. Also known as the Campus Killer, Bundy would return to his victims days later to have sex with their bodies. Bundy confessed to more than thirty killings, but his body count may exceed one hundred. Keyes read books on Bundy, studying and employing many of his monstrous techniques. Even though he gave Bundy high praise, serial killers are extremely egocentric, and Keyes was adamant that he didn't want comparisons to deflect from his own murderous achievements.

What he did next with Samantha Koenig's body put into motion a diabolical scheme that threw the Anchorage Police Department for a loop. Keyes fixed her hair, applied makeup, and sewed her eyes open with fishing line. He then took a Polaroid picture and attached it to a ransom note demanding $30,000. The photograph was purposely taken a little blurry, making it difficult to scrutinize.[34] Although it looked odd, it did force our department to reevaluate the investigation. Prior to receiving the photo, most cops, including myself, privately presumed Samantha was dead. Victims who are missing for more than a few hours, let alone weeks, rarely survive. All possibilities had to be considered as the case became more puzzling by the minute. At the time, we didn't know if Samantha's boyfriend was involved, or maybe the family, or perhaps even Koenig herself. While this may sound callous to suspect family members and loved ones, law enforcement can't assume anything and is duty bound to explore every lead.

In the end, the investigation would reveal a meticulous serial killer who had traversed America in search of potential victims. Keyes would stash "kill kits," sometimes years in advance, when planning murders. He is believed to have killed at least eleven, but there are surely more. Did he have postmortem sex with every victim? He teased law enforcement that he'd let them know everything, but Keyes took his own life in an Alaska jail cell. He

---

[34] While reenacted photographs are depicted online, the actual image has not been released to the public.

used a disposable razor blade to slit his wrists and bed sheets to strangle himself.

While I'll never shed tears for this demon's demise, it's unfortunate that he cowardly kept closure from the families of his victims by killing himself. This was his last taste of power, which he no doubt relished until his final breath. Keyes had been toying with law enforcement because in truth, he never had any intention of coming clean. To date, Samantha Koenig's dismembered body has been the only known victim recovered. While these cases don't necessarily prove a direct link between serial killers and necrophilia, history seems to have a way of repeating itself.

Bone Appétit . . .

I'm not sure if I can lighten up a topic like this, but I'll do my best. Remember those earlier percentages about male and female participation in necrophilia? Among that select group who indulged in this activity, 95 percent were male and 5 percent were female. Regardless of the numbers, it's not fair to just feature the guys here, so let's give the ladies a chance to represent. A thirty-seven-year-old woman living in Sweden, for example, allegedly found a new way to have sex with the dead.[35] Any guesses on her specific method? I'll give you a clue: she had a hankering for human bones. Police found nearly a hundred of them in her apartment. Prosecutors claimed the bones were stolen from skeletal remains and used in sexual situations, which led to charging the woman with violating the peace of the deceased. As reported by local

---

[35] Reuters, *Swedish woman charged for sexual activities with skeleton*, (Reuters, 2012). https://www.reuters.com/article/us-sweden-skeleton/swedish-woman-charged-for-sexual-activities-with-skeleton-idUSBRE8AK0IJ20121121/. Article also viewable at: dougfifer.com.

news agencies with ties to law enforcement, the investigation would uncover even more sinister evidence.

* CDs entitled "My Necrophilia" and "My First Experience."

* Selfies with the bones.

* Pictures of a morgue with an access code to the building.

* Body bag and drill.

* Internet post: "My morals set my limits and I'm prepared to take the punishment if something should happen."

Several psychological evaluations were carried out by the courts. Unsurprisingly, the results showed that she was fascinated by death. The woman was initially convicted but appealed to a higher court. Since prosecutors couldn't definitively prove she ever raided a tomb or broke into a morgue, the conviction was ultimately overturned. Would this classify as a true necrophilia case? I say it does, and I make no bones about it.

CHAPTER SIX

THE LAST CLIMAX

Urban Dictionary defines "fucked to death" in the following way: "To fuck somebody to death is to give them the biggest orgasm they have ever had in their lives." Sex to die for sounds fantastic, just not in the literal sense. Female black widows eat their partners during sperm transfer 70 percent of the time. Listen, I flat-out love sex, but doing the devil's dance with an odds-on chance of being cannibalized isn't happening. This chapter will explore those who foolishly and willingly decided to enter the spider's lair. These stories will validate Sir Walter Scott's famous line from 1808: "Oh, what a tangled web we weave, when first we practice to deceive." You might need a safe word as we exceed the boundaries of kinky and rough play. Let's plan on using "WTF," because that will be your natural inclination when these larger-than-life sexual appetites get out of hand.

The Professor's Last Lesson . . .

We'll start this one off with me acting as professor, but only in the sense of teaching you some terminology. The real professor, as you'll soon learn, won't be able to make it. It's probably fair to say you've never seen a college lesson plan quite like this one. It's also fair to say, depending on what turns you on, that this might be the most important lesson you'll ever receive. My style of lecturing is best described by a John Henrick Clarke quote: "A good teacher, like a good entertainer, first must hold his audience's attention; then he can teach his lesson." So welcome, students, to "Go Fuck Yourself," a new addition to the core curriculum.

Lesson Title:	Go Fuck Yourself		
Topic:	Autoerotic Asphyxiation		
Subject / Course:	When Self-Pleasuring Becomes Self-Sacrifice		
Lesson Cost:	Possibly Your Life	Lesson Duration:	4-6 minutes

Lesson Objectives:

Students will gain an understanding of the following:

1. The next breath in life is more important than the last (oxygen = life).

2. There is no doctor-approved way to strangle yourself while masturbating.

3. This activity may lead to serious injury, including cardiac arrest, brain damage, and death.

Summary of Tasks / Actions:
1. Define autoerotic asphyxiation.
2. What are the different types?
3. Why do you think people engage in this behavior?

Basic Materials / Equipment:	Advanced Materials / Equipment:
A healthy—or perhaps an unhealthy—imagination	Chemical substances, disco glasses, sex toys, huffing oil, mittens, vacuum
Belt, rope, wire, shoelaces, plastic bag, gas mask	Video equipment

References:
FBI statistics on autoerotic asphyxiation
David Carradine's last night in Bangkok

Bottom Line / Safety Tips:
Men: Stick to lotion for jerking off.
Ladies: Keep extra batteries on hand.

Most of us have heard the term autoerotic asphyxiation (AEA), but do we really understand what it is? The foremost authority on anything psych-related is the *Diagnostic and Statistical Manual of Mental Disorders*, better known as the DSM. This psychiatry bible lists several hundred disorders and describes the criteria and symptoms used when diagnosing psychological abnormalities. Worldwide, it is considered the authoritative guide on psychological pathologies. The DSM acts as a common language for healthcare professionals and others who commonly interact with serious mental illness. With an estimated 10 percent to 20 percent of police contacts involving mental health issues, more and more cops are being trained using the DSM guidelines. These specialized officers are part of a crisis intervention team (CIT) and respond to calls related to serious mental illness or any psychiatric crisis. This is incredibly important work, as police officers are not only the gatekeepers of the criminal justice system, but also the mental health system.

Paraphilia, in and of itself, refers to atypical sexual interest or behavior. Autoerotic asphyxiation is categorized as a paraphilic disorder. The transition to "disorder" is made when these recurrent, intense sexual urges or behaviors cause stress, humiliation, or impairment to an individual or risk of harm to others. When an individual deliberately induces hypoxia to heighten sexual gratification, this is known as autoerotic asphyxiation. I hate to oversimplify, but in most cases, it involves strangling yourself to cum harder. While this certainly doesn't qualify as a medical definition, it does get straight to the point. Now, don't worry if you like being choked a bit by your partner—it's not quite the same. That kink falls under "erotic asphyxiation" or "breath play." Autoerotic, by contrast, involves playing with your own air supply.

The DSM identifies eight major paraphilias and paraphilic disorders, and while countless others exist, these are the top dogs, clinically speaking:

1. **Exhibitionism**: "taking it out" in public

2. **Fetishism**: the pathological displacement of erotic interest and satisfaction to an object or part of the body

3. **Frotteurism**: rubbing genitals on a nonconsenting person

4. **Pedophilia**: sexual feelings toward children

5. **Sexual masochism**: sexual arousal derived from physical pain, including autoerotic asphyxiation

6. **Sexual sadism**: inflicting physical or psychological suffering on another to stimulate sexual excitement

7. **Transvestism**: cross-dressing

8. **Voyeurism**: watching naked people—for example, the "creeper cam"

That's one hell of a list, but it just scratches the surface: hundreds upon hundreds of paraphilic conditions exist. Even prior to this chapter, you are already becoming proficient in what turns someone on. You learned about coprophilia—remember the pig fucker? He couldn't become aroused without being covered in shit. How about zoophilia? Think back to the horse fucker and his sexual fixation on stallions. And then there's the dog fucker and his bestial liaisons with Lassie. We might be in some trouble as a society when I can combine pig, horse, and dog fucker into one paragraph. But before we get off the subject here, I have a few paraphilias that deserve mention, in no special order:

Crush fetish: a sexual arousal from seeing small creatures crushed. Okay . . . this one screams "serial killer."

Vorarephilia: a sexual attraction to being eaten or eating another person or creature. Again—serial killer stuff. Think Jeffrey Dahmer, a.k.a. the Milwaukee Cannibal.

Sitophilia: a sexual arousal from food. I had to offer at least one normal paraphilia here, because who doesn't like whipped cream and strawberries?

We now know the definition of autoerotic asphyxiation, but what are the different methods? They include hanging, suffocation, self-strangulation, the use of gas or solvents, and compression, to name a few. Luckily, or unluckily for you, this chapter will showcase many of these techniques. A quick rundown of how these work might be of help:

Hanging: (most common in 70 percent to 80 percent of deaths) looping a rope, belt, or string around the neck and attaching the other end to an anchor point so you can lower yourself in a controlled suspension

Suffocation: covering the mouth and nose with tape, the entire head with plastic bags, and/or even the entire body with a body-sized bag

Self-strangulation: choking yourself with your hand, or manually tightening some form of ligature around the neck, such as wire or rope

Gas or solvents: inhaling chemical agents that induce semi-consciousness

Compression: applying neck or chest pressure with the weight of some object

The primary goal here is the restriction of oxygen. Whatever accomplishes that objective qualifies, so, really, the sky's the limit as far as methodologies go. For example, you could climb to the top of Mount Everest and rub one out. The oxygen available at the highest peak is about one third that of sea level. Look at that—we've added another method to the list: altitude-induced autoerotic asphyxiation. I guess that's one way to join the Mile-High Club.

The biggest question yet to be answered: why do people engage in this type of behavior? Historically, it has been tricky to pinpoint when the practice of autoerotic asphyxiation began. Most estimates date it back to the seventeenth century, but in an *ABC News* article titled "Autoerotic Asphyxia's Deadly Thrill," it's suggested that the practice has been around a lot longer.[36] The article references the work of Stephen Hucker, a forensic psychiatrist from the University of Toronto, who is considered one of the foremost experts on this subject. According to his research, the ancient Mayans had stone statues depicting such behavior around 1,000 AD.

As for the motivations behind autoerotic behavior, it's probably safe to say that the ends justify the means. AEA is often referred to as sexual heroin due to the fact that hypoxia can create a semi-hallucinogenic state with intense feelings of happiness that is comparable to heroin use. This, coupled with the release

[36] *Auto-Erotic Asphyxia's Deadly Thrill*, (ABC News, 2009). https://abcnews.go.com/Health/story?id=7764618&page=1. Article also viewable at: dougfifer.com.

of endorphins and adrenaline, reportedly leads to a superhuman orgasm. Considering this, sexual heroin doesn't sound all that bad. With that being said, the risk of permanently kicking our oxygen habit will keep most of us on the sidelines. It's also likely the thrill of the risk adds to the pleasure of autoerotic asphyxiation. *La petite mort*, or "the little death," is a French expression referring to the glorious culminating sensation of an orgasm. Put simply, it's the brief loss or weakening of consciousness during climax. It's no wonder why Parisians are some of the busiest lovers in the world.

Okay, class, let's get into the practical application of AEA by reviewing a case study. Anchorage, Alaska, has one public university with about twelve thousand students. The college follows the academic standard of a fifteen-to-one faculty-student ratio, but that number will soon need a slight adjustment. We've all had those coworkers who never show up late, never complain, and never miss a day on the job. We'll be talking about "that guy" in this story. Let's just say his office was adorned with many prestigious faculty awards. From the outside looking in, he was the *crème de la crème* of the academic world.

Then, one day, out of the clear blue sky, his office sat empty. A colleague quickly noticed his absence, and she immediately started calling his cell phone, but there was no answer. She knew intuitively something was seriously wrong. A call to the Anchorage Police Department was followed by a mad dash to his house—not by the cops, but rather the concerned faculty member. When she arrived, at first glance, it seemed A-OK. The front door was locked, and the blinds were drawn. When no one responded to her knocking, she checked the back sliding glass doors. They were unlocked, and she went inside. Now, as a cop, I always advise citizens to wait for the police, but I get it; all she wanted to do was find her colleague and friend. Be careful what you wish for, though, because she did indeed find him, although not in the way she would have liked.

He was lying on his back, in bed, almost completely naked with his junk on full display. I say "almost naked" because he was wearing a gas mask, latex gloves, and black dress socks. Complementing the gas mask were sunglasses and headphones. What was playing in the background? None other than Mozart. A hose was connected to the mask that led to a canister filled with Amsterdam poppers, a liquid solvent containing nitrites that is often used as an inhalant. What exactly are nitrites? They are chemical compounds that contain nitrogen and oxygen, often used in prescription drugs, food preservatives, and lawn fertilizers. But poppers, when inhaled, produce a euphoric effect. They are marketed to increase libido, lower inhibitions, and improve orgasms. Another effect is the relaxation of the anal sphincter, and, oh yeah, this will enter the picture momentarily.

The U.S. Food and Drug Administration (FDA) warns consumers not to purchase or use nitrite poppers. On its website, the FDA outlines the serious health effects, which include severe headaches, dizziness, extreme drops in blood pressure, difficulty breathing, and sometimes even death. Speaking of death, the professor had taught his last lesson and popped his last popper. The investigation would show he had quite a bag of sexual tricks. On the table next to his bed was gun oil—no, not the stuff that lubricates firearms. Although called "gun oil," it's actually used as a silicone-based intimate lubricant to protect sensitive tissue from irritation and inflammation. Next to that was a product called Maximum Impact, another silicone lubricant advertising "a sensual glide." It seemed like a lot of lube for just one guy, until the medical examiner rolled him over. Once on his stomach, a monstrous dildo slowly eased out of his ass. (Remember our safe word: WTF!) This beast wanted back out, and how it fit up there in the first place is a mystery. I feel sorry for the colleague; even though she didn't see the dildo, she'll never be able to unsee the rest.[37]

As far as autoerotic asphyxiation goes, this method would fall under the gas or solvents category. But this guy had a lot more going on. His closet was filled with leather bondage gear and hardcore sex toys, indicating he also liked a little pain in his game. Combinations of paraphilias are not uncommon; in fact, police work has taught me they often go hand in hand. How many people die yearly from AEA in the United States? The FBI estimates between five hundred and a thousand. Undoubtedly, this is underreported due to the embarrassment of surviving relatives or the misidentifications of suicide. We need only look to the case of David Carradine, the famous *Kung Fu* actor who died of autoerotic asphyxiation in Bangkok, Thailand. Police initially suspected suicide, but his family wanted the FBI to investigate it as a suspicious death, possibly a homicide. He was found naked, suspended from a clothing rod in a hotel closet, with a rope tied to his neck and genitals. Video surveillance would prove he had been the sole occupant in the room. Despite this overwhelming evidence indicating AEA, the investigation would drag out for months. It's common for families to fight the findings, because AEA is understandably hard to grasp.

Before I dismiss the class, we should cover a few key points and safety tips in your lesson plan. Most importantly, there is not a doctor-approved way to strangle yourself while masturbating. The quest for the super orgasm, sexual heroin, or an exquisite

---

[37] Crime scene photos are viewable at: dougfifer.com.

la petite mort is like playing Russian roulette. The difference between death and glory can be seconds. The best advice for my teacher's pets: guys, stick with lotion, and ladies, keep extra batteries on hand.

When the Carpenter Mismeasured . . .

Being good with your wood can be a valuable skill in life. The feeling of hammering it out or pounding it hard can be very rewarding. After all, there's nothing more satisfying than reaping the fruits of your labor. Oh, wait . . . are you thinking this story is about masturbation or lovemaking? Sorry if you misunderstood, but we're going to be learning about real wood. Yup, the stuff that comes from trees.

Most of us couldn't build a house from the ground up if our lives depended on it. That takes talent well beyond our woodshop skills from high school. I hate to dash hopes, but nailing together that prefab birdhouse from Home Depot doesn't make you Bob the Builder. Want to meet the real Bob? You're in luck because introductions are forthcoming. We'll start this story by picturing the quintessential neighborhood adorned with charming houses and beautifully landscaped yards. One well-crafted residence stood out from them all. The pride of ownership was undeniable. The house boasted custom windows and doors with a sprawling front porch. It was a pad worthy of being featured in *Better Homes & Gardens*.

This guy was a magician in the carpentry world. He could build anything and perfected everything he touched. He's the guy you want to hire from Angie's List. Not only was he incredibly successful in his trade, but his business brand was booming. He was in his early thirties and owned his house free of debt.

Married with two small kiddos, by all accounts, this woodworking genius was dominating life and living the American dream.

But like so many of us, Bob had secrets. You might remember what the back of this book said: "You'll never look at your neighbor the same way." Well . . . Bob could be that neighbor. No, he wasn't dabbling in some side piece. No, he didn't have an unhealthy porn addiction. No, he wasn't into autoerotic asphyxiation. So, what was he into? When I say it's "fucked up," I mean it's really fucked up. The fetish itself is not unusual, but the methodical process he followed is nothing short of extraordinary.

This hardworking chap never missed a day of work in his life—that is, until he missed his first, which would also turn out to be his last day on Earth. His routine was normally solid, working long hours before coming home to enjoy dinner with the family. After helping with a few household chores, which included getting the kids to bed, the devoted father would retreat to his workshop to finish up projects. This wasn't a typical workshop; it was more like being in a builder's dream world. It was normal for him to spend hours each night in his happy place, and not unlike a man cave, his supportive wife rarely bothered him. He would always come to bed when he finished up.

Let's fast-forward a bit to the moment his wife wakes up without her workaholic husband in bed. His side hadn't yet been slept in, so where was he? Could he have worked straight through the night completing a project? As all wives would do, she went to look for him. He wasn't anywhere in the house and his work truck was parked in the driveway. An initial check of his shop yielded nothing. She called his cell phone, and although there was no answer, the ringing sound could be heard coming from a large box that had been built within his workshop. The odd thing about this giant box was that it didn't have any doors. It did have a ladder next to it, however, so the wife climbed up to have a look.

It would be horrific for anyone to find a loved one deceased, but the horror of finding Bob in his current condition was beyond brutal. Sadly, he had bled to death. The human body contains a lot of blood, about 1.5 gallons. How quickly you die goes hand in hand with how much blood you lose because your heart stops pumping when there's no blood left to pump. It was quite obvious that his demise had been both long and excruciating.

Why was he in the box? We'll need to delve into his fetish to understand. On second thought, understanding this one might be a stretch, so I'll just give the basic facts. Megalophilia is the sexual arousal derived from large objects and is most often associated with anal insertion. I know what you're thinking: *If you like shoving things up your ass, why build an elaborate box?* Well, the box was a part of his fetish. You see, the master carpenter had constructed a pulley system in the box, allowing him to raise and lower his suspended body. Fastened to the base was a self-made metal object awaiting his desires. It was smaller at the top, increasing in girth toward the bottom. His goal was to take the object deeper and deeper inside of him as he lowered himself with the pulleys. As you might have guessed, this fatal incident wasn't his first rodeo.

He would climb into the box from the top, completely disrobe, and fasten himself in. Up and down he would go, again and again, taking more and more of it with each drop. That is, until the pulley system unexpectedly broke loose and Bob's box turned into Bob's coffin. Impaled, he bled out slowly from the massive rectal trauma. A true carpenter's motto is "measure twice, cut once," but it's never a good idea to force the fit.

RIP Bob.

The Jizz in the Whiz . . .

Just when it seems like this chapter couldn't get any more neurotic, our next freaky fetish participant wants you to hold his beer. But before we get into his strange addiction, we should touch on a trending topic related to nearly all these cases, captured by the following question: "Why do so many of these stories involve men?" Most of the suspects in my own investigations related to atypical sexual behavior were men. Although a ton of research exists on the various disorders themselves, the prevalent involvement of men is rarely examined or discussed. Does this mean women don't partake in such risky pleasures? Absolutely not, but without a doubt, they do so far less than their male counterparts. *The American Journal of Forensic Medicine and Pathology* published an article that estimated that the autoerotic asphyxiation death rate by gender was greater than fifty to one in favor of males.[38] Cops tend to have a pretty good bird's-eye view on who's doing what in society, so from this Alaskan perspective as an investigator, I'd easily double that ratio.

Since we've established that men tend to die at a much higher rate than women during self-stimulation, it's time to see who's taking the next dirt nap in this exploration. Have you ever wanted to get down and dirty with a wet suit? Does the very thought of neoprene against your skin bring you to sexual climax? If so, welcome to "total enclosure fetishism." This is when arousal comes from having your entire body tightly enclosed in various ways. If you're claustrophobic, this may not be your kind of kink, but

---

[38] Paul D. Gosink and Mary I. Jumbelic, *Autoerotic Asphyxiation in a Female*, (The American Journal of Forensic Medicine and Pathology 21, no. 2, 2000). https://journals.lww.com/amjforensicmedicine/abstract/2000/06000/autoerotic_asphyxiation_in_a_female.4.aspx. Article also viewable at: dougfifer.com.

don't be too quick to judge. If you love cheese, things are about to get interesting. This chapter is all about the cheddar, and while I'm no cheese aficionado, I do have some rather fascinating real-life expertise.

Before we get started on this rather unique fetish, we'll need to put the super-tight wet suit wearer on the back burner for a minute. He'll be fine simmering for a bit—trust me, he's not going anywhere. First, let's consider a couple who had a sexual bucket list, a checklist of various sex acts. At first glance, thoroughness and record-keeping sound very adulting, but we should check to see what's on that wish list before we succumb to admiration. For this couple at first, having a sexual bucket list added a much-needed spark into their relationship. One by one, their must-dos were checked off.

1. Have sex in a public place

2. Watch porn together

3. Role play

4. Anal sex (with a twist)

5. Bring in a third party

Needless to say, we can stop with number five, because we all know when and where this pipe dream ends. Relationship 101 covers the explicit rule prohibiting partners from getting some strange on the side. Despite this rule being tried and true, couples will occasionally try to outsmart the universal law of human interplay. In theory, a combined consensual hookup allows both parties to take part in this forbidden fruit. If a *ménage à trois* sounds like a win-win, well, the following should save you from learning the hard way. Let's start off by teaching you the sexual connection between threesomes and cheese. To get even more specific, we'll be focusing on the category of squirt-on cheese. Think Cheez Whiz, Easy Cheese, Go Cheese, Cheese Blast!, and Cheese Wow!, to name a few brands.

You might be wondering how an Alaskan cop came across a sexually related Cheez Whiz story. As unlikely as it may seem, I don't have just one—I've got two. Yes, both of the following accounts involve processed cheese spread. Let's get back to the couple who voluntarily created a love triangle. It was initially a smashing success, no pun intended. The soon-to-be third wheel even moved in with them. Now I'm not a relationship expert, but I can tell you that this crosses healthy boundaries. Fast-forwarding to the 911 call will prove my point. I was the lucky officer to get dispatched to the residence because of a domestic dispute. A bit more information came in, and I found out the wife was upset about the husband having a girlfriend. One would think police officers hate these types of calls, but it's quite the contrary. The gossip and mudslinging between scorned lovers are better than any TV docudrama, and cops always have front row seats when all hell breaks loose.

As I pulled up to the house, it was already quite evident emotions were running high. The wife was screaming "Get the fuck out of my house!" over and over again. She was standing in the yard, yelling toward an open front door. I assumed the message was intended for her husband but later learned it was directed toward the third party. After a few minutes of calming her down, we got to the nitty-gritty real fast. She wanted the "other bitch" out of her house. She admitted they were all involved in a sexual relationship. When asked what she meant by "all," she nonchalantly laid it out. She was fucking another woman, her husband was also fucking that woman, and all three were doing it together.

To be perfectly honest here, I was mentally high fiving the husband, but being a consummate professional, I kept that part to myself. As the story unfolded, I was soon to be blown away by the circumstances leading up to this mutual fuck fest.

The couple had been married for several years and wanted to spice up their sex life. They agreed that a sexual bucket list would give them equal opportunity to explore their desires. Having sex in public was her idea, while watching porn was his. She added role playing to the list, and he added anal sex. You probably notice that number four on the list above has some additional parenthetic context. We'll get to that soon enough, but first let's tackle the big enchilada. Who selected bringing in a third party? Not surprisingly, the husband did. A *Psychology Today* article cites research suggesting 82 percent of men and 31 percent of women reported at least some interest in threesomes.[39] With roughly a three-in-ten chance, the hubby had a tall mountain to climb. At first the wife was hesitant, for obvious reasons. He was persistent, however, and persuasively suggested it would "expand their connection." He even offered to establish relationship boundaries so jealousy would not become an issue. Together, they went over the possible sexual scenarios in order to agree on what was off limits and what was acceptable. Despite the roadblocks and warning signs, this smooth operator had pulled off the impossible. She gave the green light to participate, but only if they didn't share their emotional intimacy with the third lover.

The couple initially cycled through a few prospects before landing on someone they both really liked. For several months,

---

[39] Zhana Vrangalova, *Do Most People Really Want to Have a Threesome?*, (Psychology Today, 2016). https://www.psychologytoday.com/us/blog/strictly-casual/201603/do-most-people-really-want-have-threesome. Article also viewable at: dougfifer.com.

the trio became a fine-tuned lovemaking machine. It was a sexual utopia for all. As this three-person relationship blossomed, predictably, emotions slowly seeped in. The couple had strictly agreed that neither one of them could have sex with the third lover outside of the threesome. This would soon change when the husband broke the agreement and had one-on-one relations with the new girl. To retaliate, the wife also broke the agreement by engaging in a little girl-on-girl action. If you're thinking this would be a great episode on *Jerry Springer*, you'd be spot on. To put the trust back into their relationship, there was only one thing they could think to do. No, it wasn't breaking things off with the shared lover. Instead, they invited her to live with them.

Now remember—this couple liked to plan things out and agree to terms. In their eyes, this was a smart move to avoid any miscommunication, so they did this prior to living with the other woman. Next up, they decided to have all parties sign a sexual threesome contract. Ideally, this would prevent any one of them from crossing agreed-upon boundaries. Oddly, the contract didn't include the previous prohibition of one-on-one sex. How do I know so much about this sex contract? Well, because the wife handed me a copy as evidence. It was titled "Three-Way Sex Contract and Confidentiality Agreement." This was certainly a first for me. I didn't need to read this document—it wasn't evidence—but you bet your sweet ass I took a look-see. One very specific requirement caught my eye. It stated that a certain sexual act could not be performed by the husband on the other woman. Specifically, it read, "Anal play is approved but not with anal spray." (Don't worry—I'll get to that.) Finally, the contract asserted that if emotions got out of hand or if any part of the contract was violated, then the live-in lover would have to leave. All three parties had signed and dated the contract.

In her emotional confusion, the woman who gave me the contract honestly believed that it gave me the ability to enforce it as law. Since the other woman had violated a specific constraint within the agreement, in her mind, I was duty bound to take action. She also added that emotions were out of control, which, according to the contract, mandated the girlfriend had to leave. All I could think was, *Wow, writing up a three-way sex contract is ballsy as hell!* The contract had some pedestrian rules in it, but these were coupled with some really strange stuff as well. With regard to the former, it required equal time should be spent between all parties involved. I liked that one; it seemed sensible. Dinners were to be eaten together and movies watched together. I could get on board with these too. Jealousy was absolutely prohibited. *Okay,* I thought, *now you are getting unrealistically greedy, people.* I remember smirking at how well this rule was apparently working. As for sex, I was rather surprised how much the contract allowed. Oral, vaginal, and anal intercourse were permitted between all three. What didn't make sense was the prohibition against using "anal spray" on the mistress. What in the hell is anal spray? My first thought—and don't judge me—was maybe this rule prohibited the husband from shooting his load there. Or maybe it was some type of lube. But if this were true, my next question would have to be *Why in the world does the wife care?* He's already going back door with her permission. I was dying of curiosity, but I didn't want to blurt out, "Hey, what's up with the anal play scenario?"

The wife continued to demand I arrest the other woman. I explained to her that a personal sex contract is not criminally enforceable in Alaska. She was insistent that violating a rule within a contract was an unlawful act. This was my opening to ask, "Which rule did she violate?" Without hesitation, she said,

"The anal play requirement." This led to the most unusual follow-up question of my law enforcement career: "Isn't anal play approved?" She replied, "Yes and no." Yup, I had finally arrived in Bizarro World, with no departure date in sight. Somewhat frustrated, I told her that she wasn't making any sense, and in any case, it wasn't really a police matter. What came next was a stunning admission. "Anal spray" referred to spray-on cheese. Remember that sex bucket list item with a twist? Apparently, hubby had a weakness for some cheese spread. This happened to be a fetish he embraced out of wedlock, which the wife discovered after holy matrimony. I'll just come right out with it: he liked to jack off with Cheez Whiz. Yes, you did read that right: her other half enjoyed the feeling of the processed-cheese gooeyness on his penis. She was the only person on the planet who knew about it . . . well, until now. Believe it or not, it was a form of profound intimacy between the two. Since he had confided his deepest and darkest secret to her, she felt the cheese spread was their special bond, not to be shared with anyone else.

You've probably already guessed what the "twist" was in regard to anal sex. If soft and sticky cheese feels good on your dick, *and* you also like anal, then it makes perfect sense to combine the two. The husband would insert the cheese spray nozzle into the wife's ass and fill her up. He'd still have the sensation of the cheesy sauce, coupled with some third-hole fun, which only elevated his orgasms. If this sounds a little too outrageous, I'd direct you to the World Wide Web and search the term "Whackin' it with Cheez Whiz"—you may be surprised. (On a quick side note, I highly recommend you clear your web browsing history after finishing this book.) So, why was this a no-no for the live-in lover? Because it was the couple's way of connecting on a deeper level, and the wife felt emotionally secure knowing it was the one sex act that could not be shared. In the contract, she literally "cut the cheese" from the mistress's permissions. In spite of this, our ladies' man turned out to be more of a "sharing is caring" kind of guy. Unable to resist the temptation, he ended up reverting to old habits.

Only this time, the hubby's royal fuckup would end their marriage. Luckily for him, apps like 3Fun, 3way, and 3Somer are exploding in growth. Most of these sites advise members to be upfront and honest with potential partners. I'm not sure exactly what his pickup line should be, but let's hope he doesn't make it too cheesy.

Wait a minute—this chapter is "The Last Climax," but the couple didn't die? Remember, I don't have just one cheesy story—I've got two. Rest assured, the angel of death will be collecting our next soul, so let's get back to that hold-my-beer guy I mentioned earlier. I'd like to introduce you to Wet Suit Willy. It might seem rather odd to quote Shakespeare at this moment, but hear me out. "What's in a name?" is a famous line in the tragic love story of *Romeo and Juliet*. It signifies that a name can never truly define you as a person. Unless, of course, you're Wet Suit Willy, whose nickname could not have been more fitting—it was literally dead on. And strangely enough, this too will be a tragic love story, albeit much less romantic.

To be a top-notch cop, you need to keep abreast of the latest and greatest investigation techniques. Crime scene analysis is clearly key to our jobs. Examples include fingerprinting, DNA collection, photography, blood spatter analysis, identification of trace evidence—the list goes on and on. Over the years I've taken class after class on nearly every police training course imaginable, from how to investigate homicides to hostage negotiations. Out of all of them, one training stands out. The course was called

Deviant Sexual Behavior and Related Criminal Activity. This is where I met Wet Suit Willy.

To set the stage properly, this wasn't an in-the-flesh meeting because poor Willy had already kicked the bucket. So how did he and I meet? Forensic photography would bring him back to life before me. Not like Jon Snow's reawakening in *Game of Thrones* but rather through a reconstruction of events using visual aids. Forensic photography dates to the late nineteenth century. Although you wouldn't guess it, photography as a crime-solving tool remains second to none. Throughout history, this technology has put more criminals behind bars than any other investigative technique. But, you might ask, what about deoxyribonucleic acid, better known as DNA? Isn't this the poster child of modern-day evidence? We can settle this by way of illustration because if you really think about it, you can't become a poster child without first taking a picture.

Every photo has a story to tell, and when these images are linked to criminal activity, it's vitally important police investigators play the part of storytellers who can annotate this imagery. I have sat on the witness stand in front of numerous juries with only photos in hand, unlocking these frozen moments in time with my testimony. In order to become an expert in any field, you must devote time to professional development. You've probably heard of the ten-thousand-hour rule, which is the magic number needed to achieve expertise. Whether that figure is true or not, I've spent more than fifty thousand hours working and training as a cop. While this doesn't necessarily make me an expert, it does give me the ability to tell one hell of a story based on forensic photography.

And that was my assigned training scenario while attending the class on deviant sexual behavior and related criminal activity:

tell the story of what happened. Using only crime scene photographs, I was tasked with unraveling the mystery and finding the truth. So, it's about time we blow Wet Suit Willy's cover by using the four Ps of storytelling: people, place, plot, and purpose.

People. Characters are what make stories good. We've already established who the big cheese is here.

Place. This is the scene of the crime. In this case, it's a dirty apartment with dirty little secrets.

Plot. This is where the main character is put into a challenging situation. We'll focus on the incident, dilemma, and climax. Briefly, Wet Suit Willy had a total enclosure fetish, went too far with it, and died.

Purpose. This explains why the story is important and why others will care. In this case, it's because the truth is perverted, disgusting, and unimaginable, yet this will only draw you in more.

The first photograph showed a dingy little studio apartment. It was filthy, with garbage, food, and clothing scattered everywhere. A heavily stained carpet added to the nastiness. The lack of furniture was curious—there was no couch or bed. The next picture showed several spray cans of cheese laying on the soiled carpet. Finally, saving the best for last, there was the shocking image of Wet Suit Willy himself. He was positioned on his back, lying on the carpet and wearing—you guessed it—a wet suit. The body looked heavily bloated, as if the wet suit was about to burst. From an investigative standpoint, this bloat is important in order to potentially set a decomposition timeline. Although environmental factors can speed up or delay the onset of decomposition, the general rate of decay has been well established. Are you wondering how fast we rot postmortem?

Twenty-four to seventy-two hours after death: internal organs decompose.

Three to five days after death: the body starts to bloat and foam, containing blood leaks from the mouth and nose.

Eight to ten days after death: the body turns from green to red as the blood decomposes and the organs in the abdomen accumulate gas.

Several weeks after death: nails and teeth fall out.

One month after death: the body starts to liquefy.[40]

I can attest that this is, without a doubt, as nasty as it sounds. I have seen and—what's even worse—*smelled* all of these. After studying the three photos relating to Wet Suit Willy's demise, did I solve this whodunit? Not even close—but I did wow the instructors by pinpointing when the death occurred. The extreme bloating, I thought, was a dead giveaway: the deceased had passed approximately three to five days prior. To my surprise, however, my reasoning based on visual evidence was not entirely correct; it turned out Wet Suit Willy was not bloated at all. Additional photographs would show he was wearing not one, not two, but three extremely tight wet suits. He was puffed up all right . . . with neoprene. When the wet suits were cut from his body, some

---

[40] *The Stages of Human Decomposition*, (EXIT Biohazard & Crime Scene Cleanup, 2021). https://www.exitcleanup.com/the-stages-of-human-decomposition. Article also viewable at: dougfifer.com.

unexpected matter was found. Don't lie: you went straight to semen, didn't you? Well, we'll get to that soon, but first up will be the Cheez Whiz. Yes, remember those cans of gooey goodness on the carpet? Willy liked a complete layer of cheese spread in between each wet suit. And our boy wasn't shy with his supply: the thickest layer was caked directly on his skin, entombed by wet suit number one.

By all accounts, Willy wasn't a scuba diver, and he didn't like surfing, but he did like very snug synthetic rubber against his skin. After somehow wiggling into wet suit number three, his life would cease to be. It was so tight against his chest that his breathing was almost completely restricted. He undoubtedly struggled to free himself but eventually succumbed to positional asphyxia caused by his total enclosure fetishism. Let's return to your first thought about semen being found—you were right. By enclosing his entire body, he was so sexually aroused that before losing all mobility, Willy was able to practice some self-love. Recall that the apartment was never cleaned—suffice it to say, neither was his neoprene.

The Lethal Leotard . . .

Sex, pleasure, orgasm, repeat—this sequence is an undeniable force of nature that dominates most of our lives, but how much is mental and how much is physical? The following case might give you a new perspective on just how powerful the mind is. The "big O" certainly feels physical, but in truth, your brain is the most powerful sex organ.

Keeping your eye on the prize is typically a good thing, although the following set of circumstances will bring a whole new meaning to this expression. Even in my experience, this was a peculiar investigation. Picture a six-foot-six-inch male dressed only in a leotard with thick purple mittens duct-taped around his wrists. He had a long, black wig on and was hanging by the neck in front of a full-length mirror. Yup, he was dead as a door-nail. Displayed around the room were hundreds of photographs showing the same man in various states of dress. Many showed him actively masturbating while staring intently into the mirror. In one rather displeasing photo, he was wearing a Superman singlet with the penis area cut out. His pocket rocket was fully erect, and he was smiling like there was no tomorrow. I suppose the smile was a little prophetic.

I didn't need to ask myself what happened; I knew immediately. The front part of the leotard that cupped his crotch area was soaked. Nope, he didn't pee himself while hanging; it was seminal fluid. I'd been at a variety of similar autoerotic deaths, but this one had a unique twist. Typically, the victim has access to their genitals for self-gratification, but in this case, it would have been impossible for the male to grab his penis. First off, the leotard was about three times too small, making the crotch area snug as a bug. Secondly, the mittens were thick and without fingers.

So how did he cum? He kept his eye on the prize. The mere act of viewing himself in the mirror, dressed in a leotard, wig, and mittens was enough to have an orgasm. "Impossible," you say? Oh, it's not only possible, but science agrees as well. Remember those nocturnal emissions, better known as wet dreams? These sleep orgasms are not caused by masturbation during sleep; they occur without any manual stimulation. Although this phenomenon most often occurs in puberty, both men and women are capable of wet dreams throughout their lives. On top of that, a recent case report published in *The Journal of Sexual Medicine* focused on a thirty-three-year-old woman who can reach orgasm without any genital contact. To prove this, the study measured her hormone levels, which were elevated and consistent with orgasms induced by "hands-on" clitoral stimulation. I guess, in some cases, getting mind fucked isn't so bad after all.

So, how did the man in mittens die? It was purely by accident. A nail in the ceiling held the other end of the rope around his neck. The ceiling had thirty to forty holes, which indicated he had done this many times before. Wondering how it works? You lean into the rope as you fantasize, which starts the restriction of oxygen. Ninety-nine percent of the time, the nail pulls out from the weight of your body falling forward after you pass out. But the 1 percent of times when it doesn't, you're literally fucked.

Let's get back to that collage of photos for a moment. Prior to this call, I was a huge *Superman* fan, and I still would be were it not for that disturbing image of the victim in the crotchless onesie being seared into my memory forever. This guy took the Man of Steel to a whole new level. But why so many pics of himself? As it turns out, he was most likely autosexual. According to family members, he had no known partners except himself. Yes, an autosexual person is sexually attracted to themselves. WebMD defines "autosexuality" as a sexual condition in which people are more attracted to themselves than to others, often preferring masturbation to sex with a partner.

I'd say banging yourself epitomizes safe sex, but keeping your eye on the prize too long turned out to be this Superman's kryptonite.

Riding Harleys and Hoovers . . .

The throaty growl of a Harley motorcycle when you peg the throttle wide open is unmistakable. And speaking of pegging, "getting pegged" is all about the excitement of pushing those limits. Thrill seekers, get ready to jump on that hog, but, fellas, hop on the back this time, because you'll be riding bitch in this story. Wondering why your man card is being revoked? It's because we'll be exploring the sexual side of pegging where the rules of engagement reverse traditional roles. You see, this is when a woman penetrates a man's anus with a strap-on dildo. If you're into it, a lil' butt action between lovers seems harmless enough. That is . . . until you combine Harleys and Hoovers.

More than three million people ride Harleys in the U.S. One of the most notorious motorcycle gangs, the Hells Angels, requires members to ride Harley-Davidson almost exclusively. Also known as "H.A.," it's the largest criminal enterprise for outlaw bikers. They have around 3,500 members worldwide with 467 chapters in fifty-nine countries. Alaska has two chapters, one in Anchorage and the other in Fairbanks. A longtime boss of the Hells Angels, Ralph "Sonny" Barger, once described the organization as "a bunch of fun-loving guys who just ride motorcycles."[41] He must have forgotten about his long list of criminal charges, including a conviction for conspiracy to violate federal law to commit murder.

The Anchorage Police Department has arrested a substantial number of H.A. members over the years for criminal acts.

---

[41] Albert De Amicis, *Hell's Angels Criminal Enterprise* (research report, University of Phoenix School of Criminal Justice Administration, 2009), Abstract, National Criminal Justice Reference Service. https://www.ojp.gov/ncjrs/virtual-library/abstracts/hells-angels-criminal-enterprise. Article also viewable at: dougfifer.com.

No surprise here—dope-related charges, predominantly meth-amphetamine, lead the list. For good measure, we can throw in extortion, trafficking stolen goods, prostitution, and violent assaults. On top of that, Alaska has unsolved homicides likely attributed to these "fun-loving guys who just ride motorcycles." Despite the murder and mayhem, I will give them a little credit on how they organize a hit. The word on the street is the Hells Angels have very specific guidelines when eliminating someone. Typically, they'll send an out-of-state enforcer to the problem area and whack the unsuspecting individual. As soon as it's done, they leave that state, never to be seen again. The enforcer is not locally known, has one job to do, and leaves as quickly as he came. Is this a recipe for a perfect murder?

Let's take a look at how most homicides are solved:

1. Suspect is intimate with or somehow connected to the victim.

2. Eyewitness recognizes the suspect.

3. Suspect talks or brags about the crime.

4. Forensic evidence, such as ballistics or DNA, implicates a suspect.

If the H.A. do, in practice, follow such a systematic process involving an outside enforcer, it would make solving these cases very difficult. The suspect wouldn't be linked to the victim. A local eyewitness cannot recognize who they don't know. The H.A. have a strict code of silence, so bragging about criminal acts rarely happens. If the evidence is professionally disposed of, this means the cops can't process what they never find. A motto associated with the Hells Angels states, "When we do it right, no one remembers." Does this mean every member of the Hells Angels is a criminal? Of course not, but not all of them are angels either.

Aside from the Hells Angels, why do over three million Americans love riding these seven-hundred-pound pieces of steel? Harley-Davidson is more than a bike; it's a lifestyle with a rallying cry of "live to ride, ride to live." This all-American icon screams "fuck you" to the traditional nine-to-five rat race, portraying true personal freedom as an open road. While Harleys are cool as hell, it's about time we shift gears and find out what's up with the Hoover. You'll need to bear with me here, as this one will take a bit of explaining. To clarify, we're talking about a top-of-the-line vacuum cleaner, not just any old dustbuster. Hoover was once the number-one-selling vacuum in America, with millions still in households today. With some of the best suction power in the industry, this bad boy got the job done. Needless to say, some people tend to push the limits on product capabilities. Are the puzzle pieces starting to come together for you yet? Maybe you're thinking that somebody used the suction part for a penis-vacuum playdate, or maybe they tried shoving the hose up their ass. Fair guesses, for sure, and Pornhub's videos confirm the unconventional use of vacuums in both bodily regions, but in this instance, neither the suction nor the hose come into play.

In fact, only the handle was involved in this deadly scandal—that's right, the *handle* of the vacuum cleaner. Since you're probably a little confused, I'll do my best to break it down for you. The owner of the Hoover, who was also a Hells Angel, took his pledge to ride or die all the way seriously. Upon his untimely death, he was wearing a black leather vest depicting his allegiance to the club. It was adorned with various patches, including the death's head logo signifying his full-fledged membership. H.A.

vests are considered sacred, and members are expected to always protect and honor them. I should also mention that that's *all* he was wearing. He was, in addition, a rather big boy, sporting three hundred pounds of body weight. Being naked in a leather vest was not a good look for him.

So, who was our rather Rubenesque rider? Surprisingly, he happened to be quite the badass biker by day, while by night, he indulged in an unusual pegging fetish. His street cred had earned him a high-ranking position within the Hells Angels. He was as gruff and tough as they come, the type you would avoid direct eye contact with at a bar. And after he died—you'll soon learn how—I would have preferred avoiding direct eye contact with his corpse as an investigator. Based on what we found, it soon became evident that besides the straightforward pegging, he also liked autoerotic asphyxiation. Think of it like peanut butter and jelly—one is good, but both together are usually better.

His *modus operandi* was to fasten a belt around his neck for the autoerotic portion of his sex act. After feeding the belt into a loop, he secured the buckle portion to the upper frame of a living room closet. Since he was heavy, he had to firmly secure it. The buckle had a clip mechanism hooked to an eye bolt. Autoerotic asphyxiation has some dos and don'ts, but in most cases, the person will attach a belt or rope to something that won't support their entire weight. This could be a small nail or a hanging rod that will break away. The most common practice is to restrict breathing while standing or kneeling, but Biker Boy had a rather unusual method. As a matter of fact, it was the only time I'd ever seen it. He was squatting on a dining room chair, bare ass at the top, leaning forward into the closet. The belt was securely fastened around his neck with his enormous belly hanging down about halfway to the floor.

As if this wasn't disturbing enough, it's time to introduce the Hoover. Now, this part took some planning and measuring. The vacuum had an angled handle that the victim had positioned behind the back of the chair, leaving about six inches cresting the top, which made it accessible for pegging pleasure. Yes, he rode that vacuum handle up and down while simultaneously asphyxiating and pleasuring himself. When he passed out and the belt didn't give, this also assured the end of his life.

Cops call it DRT, which means "dead right there." He appeared oddly frozen in time on the chair. In case you were wondering, yes, the vacuum handle was still up his ass after death. The investigation showed that his death had been purely accidental. Due to his hefty size, normal nails had previously failed to hold the belt in place, so he had picked some stronger hardware to hold his bulk just a bit longer while he finished his fun. The only problem was that the more secure anchor point never broke free after he lost consciousness, which guaranteed his death. In police work, we find organ donors in the aftermath of motorcycle crashes, but not usually propped on chairs with a Hoover vacuum handle up their ass. I do find it a little ironic that Hoover's campaign slogan once was: "Deep down, you want a Hoover."

CHAPTER SEVEN

TEACHABLE TIDBITS

By now, we've probably established your sex life is far from being deviant. More likely, you're much closer to plain old vanilla sex than you previously thought. But if you still have the urge to get your freak on from time to time without dying or going to prison, the following options can help spice things up. While traditional opportunities exist, such as hiring a certified sex coach or attending a couple's sex retreat, keep in mind that both options will set you back some serious coin. I've got a better solution, code-named "Teachable Tidbits." You've already paid the cost of admission and come this far, so here are a few naughty nuggets you can add to your personal bag of tricks—or not.

The Oracle . . .

Intellectual growth should commence at birth and cease only at death.

~Albert Einstein~

We have all heard the adage, "You can't teach an old dog new tricks."

We've also been told the polar opposite: "You're never too old to learn."

Which one rings true?

Let's look to science for the answer. Austrian and Hungarian cognitive biologists tackled this very question by testing 265 dogs of various ages. Each pooch had to push their snouts against a touchscreen display; if they selected the correct image, they received a treat. Well, the old tail waggers came through with flying colors. And believe it or not, older dogs performed better during logic-based testing.[42] So, yes, you can teach an old dog new tricks. What about us humans? Are we as capable as our canine counterparts? According to a 2021 *Popular Science* article, we thrive on neural stimulation as we age.[43] Kristen Kennedy, a cognitive neuroscientist, claims we can alter our neurons with new information and experiences "as long as we are alive and functioning." Since you are presently reading this book, I will presume that you meet these minimum qualifications. As I lay the groundwork for the following Teachable Tidbits, remember that you'll need to be open to new ideas—after all, it's good for the brain.

With over three hundred million sold in the U.S. every year, a common product found in most homes has been repurposed for the bedroom by resourceful and sexually adventurous lovers,

---

[42] David Freeman, *Scientists Prove Old Dogs Can Learn New Tricks. Here's Why That's a Good Thing,* (MACH NBC News, 2018). https://www.nbcnews.com/mach/science/computer-training-dogs-could-help-stop-old-canines-decline-ncna846066.
[43] Erin Blakemore, *Old Dogs Need to Learn New Tricks. Here's Why,* (Popular Science, 2021). https://www.popsci.com/story/science/learning-new-things-when-old/. Articles also viewable at: dougfifer.com.

proving that it's never too late to learn a new trick. Believe me when I say that this will literally blow your mind. Together, we have encountered some off-the-charts neurotic behavior while reading this book, 99 percent of which we'd run from in real life. Having said that, I'm here to welcome you to the one-percenter club. I'm an official card-carrying member of this secret society, and for less than a dollar, you can be too. Heroin addicts often call their first high "getting their wings"—once you try it, you cannot deny it. Fortunately for us, unlike heroin users, we'll skip collapsed veins, heart infections, hepatitis, and death. In fact, it is nearly impossible to overdose on this act. As we move ahead, you should be mindful of a quote by the Russian writer Anton Chekhov, "Knowledge is of no value unless you put it into practice."

Being a patrol cop, pounding the pavement, is unlike any other profession. As I've said before, I wouldn't trade in my experiences for any other calling. You can't get one "Aha!" moment after another any place else. Cops are always ready for the next call, and this one would prove to be a doozy. In ancient Greece, dating back as early as 2000 BC, decisions of any significance were guided by the hand of infallible authority figures. They were called oracles, prophets of the ancient world. Trusted and believed to be all-knowing, oracles were consulted in areas of law, military operations, governmental affairs, and personal matters. Greek mythology divided the oracles' messages into one of four methods by which the prophecy became known: orally, by signs, by dreams, or through the dead. The five oracles of ancient Greece were Dodona, Cumae, Trophonius, Erythaea, and Delphi. The last of these five, also known as Pythia, is probably the most well-known. She was the high priestess of the temple of Apollo at the sanctuary of Delphi.

Need me to dial down the history lesson a tad? We'll simplify it and take a more pragmatic approach using a relatable analogy. It's actually quite easy—think of your wife or significant other when it's decision-making time. After all, your partners are oracles in the truest sense. Want to play golf? First, find out what your oracle has to say about it. Want to buy a new toy? What does your oracle have to say about that? Let's face it—if you have any future plans whatsoever, better check with your oracle beforehand.

Going back to my patrol cop story, I could never have imagined when I showed up for my shift that I would have the opportunity to cross paths with a present-day oracle. The odds of hitting the Powerball jackpot are probably better, and Lottery USA puts those at around one in 292.2 million. Luckily for me, at this moment in time, the stars aligned. I would not only meet this person face-to-face, but also have the honor of adding a sixth mighty oracle to the history books. I would like to introduce you to Andrew, minister of magic in the sanctuary of the Last Frontier. Using our ancient oracle types above, we'll place Andrew in the first category: oral oracles.

It started off as a simple disturbance between two roommates who also turned out to be lovers. To add a little extra spice to their conflict, alcohol was involved, as it often is. If you are wondering which drug wreaks the most havoc on society, take it from a cop—one stands well above the others. If you combined the crimes related to cocaine, cannabis, hallucinogens, inhalants, ketamine, methamphetamine, and fentanyl, they still wouldn't come close to those involving liquor. We learn early in our police training that the almighty liquid courage will figure prominently in our endeavors to keep the peace. National statistics place its role in violent crimes at nearly 40 percent of all offenses.[44] For domestic violence incidents, the World Health Organization estimates 55 percent of abuse is related to alcohol.[45] Fortunately, in this particular incident, we just had intoxicated partners who needed a cooling-off period.

This is about as simple and common as it gets; it's Copland 101. Two officers respond in order to separate the subjects involved, a simple solution allowing them the opportunity to live to fight another day. We like to call this scenario a win-win: everybody remains safe, and we skip all the bullshit. In this case, as we progress into the call, we'll be disclosing an individual's sexuality. It's a key part of the story and not intended as anything more. You're probably thinking, *We've already covered horse fucking, so it's a little too late for soft-pedaling now.* I agree, so if you happen to be offended by a small detail, I'd politely suggest you slow your roll. Andrew, our oracle in this story, is gay, and he was expressly proud and forthcoming about his orientation. So much so, as we'll soon learn, he even quipped about the downsides of heterosexuality.

As the other officer and I knocked on the apartment door, we could clearly hear yelling that profanely rivaled the mouth of a sailor. To overcome the noise of the fracas, we had to ever so slightly increase the intensity of our tap at the door. We followed this with an assertive, "This is the Anchorage Police Department!" In an instant, the door was flung wide open with the following

[44] *Alcohol-Related Crimes*, (Alcohol Rehab Guide, 2023). https://www.alcoholrehabguide.org/alcohol/crimes/.
[45] *Alcohol and Domestic Abuse*, (Alcohol Rehab Guide, 2023). https://www.alcoholrehabguide.org/alcohol/crimes/domestic-abuse/.
Articles also viewable at: dougfifer.com.

welcome: "Come on in!" The male subject did not politely wait around; he was immediately back in the living room screaming at his partner. At this precise moment, our job is to separate the battling parties. Once that small feat is accomplished, we can identify what is going on and offer solutions. Sometimes cops are just a Band-Aid, but sometimes we prevent life-changing tragedies. This appeared to be a Band-Aid type of call, a verbal domestic with no crimes committed.

I asked one of the males, who turned out to be Andrew, to step into the hallway with me. The other officer stayed in the living room talking with the second individual. As a safety tactic, cops will always keep each other within eyesight until a situation is defused. That way, if things go sideways, we can immediately spring into action. Andrew, although upset about his significant other, was quite chill with me. After a long night of drinking, tempers had flared over some prior promiscuous behavior. Andrew suspected his partner was still cheating on him and wanted to be done with the relationship. Not to sound rude or uncaring, but this common situation for cops is "same crap, different rap." I would see this precise scenario reenacted a thousand times in my career. Aside from different people and addresses, it was like reliving the same experience over and over again, my very own *Groundhog Day*.

Despite it being cut and dry, we still had to resolve the matter at hand: two heavily intoxicated lovers living in the same apartment. We couldn't leave because as emotions rise, so does the likelihood of violence. I asked Andrew if he'd be willing to go somewhere else for the night. I rationalized with him that because of the drinking, tension, and alleged cheating, this was a practical solution to avoid any bad results. Usually that first soft-serve approach gets an awkward, "No chance in hell, this is my house too." But as I keep reminding you, Andrew the oracle wasn't a typical dude. Oddly enough, he agreed, but not before expressing a few departing expletives at his two-timing soon-to-be ex.

This is where things got a little more interesting. When one party agrees to leave for the night, standard protocol includes allowing them to gather up some items. After all, we all need clothes, toiletries, and whatever else we deem important for a short time away. I was always very cognizant of giving the individual an appropriate amount of time. Our training dictated fifteen minutes, but I'd give them as much time as they needed. I wouldn't like being without my personal stuff, so out of courtesy, I wanted to make sure they had theirs. With safety in mind, we follow the individual around as guns and knives can be easily concealed. We watch their every move, and for the sake of transparency, we explain the process and reasoning behind it to make it a little less off-putting.

Andrew was totally cool with it; he couldn't have cared less about his personal space being encroached upon. He grabbed a large, green military duffle bag for his belongings. His first stop—and the most common in this familiar ritual—was the bathroom. Andrew collected the customary toothbrush, toothpaste, brush, and a few other incidentals. Next up, he made a beeline to the bedroom. Obviously, most people in this situation grab clothes, blankets, and in some cases, even their pillow. Andrew opened the bottom drawer of his bedside dresser. He grabbed a few pairs of socks, T-shirts, and underwear. Being a cop, you almost feel like a creeper in these moments. You need to be uncomfortably close in order to see what they are grabbing. Accessing a gun takes a split second, and in Alaska, nearly 65 percent of residents own at least one. But when Andrew opened the top drawer of the dresser, I was perplexed by what I saw. It was completely filled from side to side with a rather unusual bedroom commodity. Any guesses? Invented in the 1800s, they are a staple during cold and flu season and most likely reside in your house today—we're talking about cough drops.

Don't worry; I'll explain soon enough. But for now, I'll assume that none of you were guessing cough drops—dozens and dozens of perfectly stacked nine-piece packages. How do I know the exact number of pieces per pack? We'll get to that Teachable Tidbit later. The drawer contained the gamut of flavors: honey-lemon, strawberry, cherry, peppermint, citrus, and Mentho-Lyptus. Without missing a beat, Andrew started stuffing them into his bag, handful by handful. I remember thinking, *What on God's green Earth is happening?* Cops by nature tend to be inquisitive, and I certainly wasn't going to miss out on this curiosity. With a shade of sarcasm, I asked Andrew, "Do you have a bad cough or something?"

As he continued piling the cough drops into his bag—every package, mind you—Andrew asked, "You don't know what these are for?" As I struggled for an answer—*any* answer—Andrew was kind enough to clue me in. He casually explained that you pop a cough drop into your mouth before performing oral sex. The menthol within the drop heats up the shaft of the penis, culminating in a more intense ejaculation. He referred to it as a "blowdrop" and warned me not to get greedy by using more than one at a time. Andrew said two cough drops used simultaneously, especially the menthol-flavored, can be more than most men can handle. It was at this moment that I felt a little self-conscious and embarrassed, a rarity in the uniform. To get back to some sort of normal conversation, I told Andrew that I wouldn't be needing any more life hacks relating to cough drops.

The next question out of Andrew's mouth was, "You don't like blow jobs?" Although I should have seen this question coming, I was thrown off a bit. I also wasn't going to touch personal inquiries into my sex life during a call with a ten-foot pole. Andrew then pointed toward my wedding ring and asked, "Does she like giving blow jobs?" Cops usually control the conversation, but in this case, the tables had turned. Andrew wouldn't stop; his liquid courage was alive and well. He wanted to know if I'd ever tried anything other than missionary position. Andrew kept going, voicing his opinion that heterosexual couples could learn a lot from homosexual couples. He told me not to worry—he'd be more than happy to share some of his naughty knowledge. I wasn't sure what rabbit hole I was now trapped in, but I was becoming more awkwardly shy by the minute. Talking about oral sex, let alone with a citizen during a call, was not on my radar for the day. I remember telling myself, *Get it together, Fifer—you're the cop here!*

The best that I could muster, after getting mildly mind-fucked, was to tell Andrew to finish getting his stuff. Always compliant, he did just that. Thinking back, I remember that it was a slow and uncomfortable walk to the front door. We were finally done with the call. I thanked Andrew for his cooperation, and he thanked me for being professional. As he departed, Andrew glanced back with a self-assured smile and said, "I had a prophecy you will enjoy it." I thought to myself, *Enjoy what? He can't seriously be talking about the cough drops.* I'm not into blowdrops; I didn't even know what a blowdrop was before this call. And who in their right mind talks in terms of prophecies? Wouldn't that require you to be a prophet? To say the least, this was bizarre. And of course, my police counterpart picked up on the offbeat goodbye, asking me afterward what I was going to enjoy. I gave him a brief recap of the conversation. He was a little shocked:

"Get the fuck outta here—a cough drop?" Putting us back in the rabbit hole, my fellow officer asked how exactly it heats up the shaft. I was suddenly the resident expert on blowdrops. Cops tend to talk to other cops in direct terms, so I politely responded, "Listen, smartass, how am I supposed to know?"

It was refreshing getting back to the sanctity of my patrol car. I could gather my thoughts, recharge my fragile mental batteries, and get on with work. Before going back in service, my partner pulled up to my vehicle and rolled his window down. In cop language, we call this 10-5-ing. This code means to meet up and talk. It's fairly routine, and discussions vary from our favorite burger joint to whose fantasy football team is playing better. He wasn't there for small talk, however. He just asked the million-dollar question: "Are you going to tell your wife about the prophecy?" Before I could say anything, he quickly drove off with a shit-eating grin.

Cops' wives, especially mine, like hearing about the freakier side of society. I knew this was worthy of a call home, with the standard declaration, "You're not going to believe this one." Kim was all ears and quite intrigued by this new revelation. She reasoned it made perfect sense that menthol cough drops would increase sensitivity by triggering the cold-sensitive receptors in the skin. First of all, it's my penis, and I didn't even know it had cold receptors. Secondly, when did my wife become a biochemist? Before hanging up, Kim matter-of-factly said, "We ought to try it sometime." Now, I know what you are thinking: I should flip on those lights and sirens and head to the nearest local drug store. And you know what? Your judgment is impeccable.

Does it work? I can tell you, without reservation, it's flat out the best oral sex I've ever had. Better yet, Kim, the aspiring biochemist, was not done with her infinite wisdom. She said since it worked for me, it should work for her as well. She cautioned that we should start with half a cough drop for her. Apparently, the clitoris has more nerve endings than any other part of the human body—in fact, twice as many as the penis. As far as Kim's results went . . . well, a gentleman doesn't kiss and tell. I will confess that cough drops are now a staple of our bedroom—both in whole and half sizes.

I can't help but reflect upon what Andrew had said regarding the number of cough drops. He warned me not to get greedy. He was quite prescient in his wisdom, as human behavior is driven by basically three things. Einstein summed it up perfectly: "There are three great forces in the world: stupidity, fear, and greed." We have all experienced and succumbed to each one of these at some point in our lifetimes. The cough drop revelation, by now, had gone viral within the police department. The officer that responded to the call with me—yup, he couldn't wait to tell me later on that he had punched his cough drop card. The number of calls I received from fellow cops, asking me about how it's done, was rather ridiculous. It's amazing that simply putting a cough drop into your mouth and going to town needed any explanation, but apparently it did. I'm not going to lie; I oddly felt some sort of power in being the expert on blowdrop proficiency. I mean, holy shit, I had become the resident expert, after all. The recipe I passed along was quite simple.

How to Make a Blowdrop:

Ingredient List: Cough drop

Directions: Have partner keep it in the mouth during oral sex

Warning: Do not exceed one cough drop per session

I was suddenly the "bad boy" of the department. Although cough drops are perfectly legal, I felt like a rule breaker. But there was one question I was continually asked: "Why only one cough drop?" I wanted to say, "Because Andrew said not to get greedy," but cops won't accept hearsay. In a legal forum, hearsay is testimony from an under-oath witness reciting an out-of-court statement. In most courts, it is inadmissible as evidence. To keep up with my newfound persona, I would need firsthand knowledge. So, I speculated that if one cough drop was life-altering, maybe—just maybe—two would curl the toes even more.

You guessed it—Kim was in. We both rationalized that pushing your boundaries in life is necessary for growth. This was my time to shine, and I was in seventh heaven. *Get ready to take a ride on the wild side*, I told myself. *We're doubling down, with nirvana as our next stop . . .* fast-forward a bit—*Oh no, I fucked up!* I'd like to introduce you to the frenulum; it's the skin flap on the underside of a penis near the opening where you pee. There is a nervous system pathway between the spinal cord and that precise spot that rapidly sends signals to the part of the nervous system that controls ejaculation. Who knew? That's how every male's Mini-Me works. Think of it as a gentleman's G-spot, an erogenous zone that contains an abundance of sensory nerve terminals, which are very susceptible to heat. In theory, doubling the cough drop dosage should have been money; instead, it buckled my knees, and I had to take a break from my honey. While I had the opposite experience in this case, the frenulum is also an area that contributes to premature ejaculation. It's safe to say that my unit wouldn't be discharging its duties on this day.

I can honestly admit that I'd never before tapped out while receiving oral sex, but if this had been a UFC match, it was lights out. Intense burning in your nether region will get the best of anyone. I wasn't predicting a spur-of-the-moment run into the bathroom, but a cold washcloth had never felt so good. With Kim laughing and me squirming, I couldn't help but think about Andrew. (Simmer down; the thoughts were purely platonic.) He had earned his title; his prophecy had come true, and Andrew the oracle had arisen. I would never see him again; I'm not sure where he's at or what he's up to. But I will always remember his rather pompous smile as we parted ways, with his words still echoing: "You'll enjoy it." I didn't have the forethought to thank Andrew back then, so I hope that somehow divine intervention gets him a copy of this book. On behalf of an entire police department and couples everywhere, Andrew, you are greatly appreciated.

Let's take a safety moment. After all, cops are all about protection. I'm not an oracle like Andrew, but I'll bet you'll be visiting the drug store soon. It would be nearly impossible to overdose on cough drops, although it might get a little hot—reaching the promised land sometimes takes a little sacrifice. The active ingredient in cough drops is menthol, mainly sourced from peppermint oil, which creates the cool and warm sensations. A typical cough drop has roughly three to ten milligrams of menthol. A lethal dose is estimated at around a thousand milligrams per kilogram of body weight. That's good news, because if you weighed 150 pounds, you'd have to eat nearly seven thousand cough drops in a short amount of time to cause a lethal overdose. And one more fun fact: there are no known cases of death from overdosing on menthol cough drops.

It's time for a moral compass check. Acquiring your blow-drop wings might trouble the conscience for some of you. This rite of passage requires that you throw, or more accurately, *blow* caution to the wind. Let's look at a few pros and cons that might help you with that decision.

PROS:

1. Entry fee minimal (great bang for the buck)
2. Keto friendly (sugar-free)
3. Vegetarian friendly (zero meat)
4. Meat eaters nonetheless encouraged (in a roundabout way)
5. Low calories (in general, around ten)
6. Gluten free (no wheat, barley, or rye)
7. Vegan (free of animal products)
8. Unisex (all private parts welcome)
9. Safe (however, double dose at your own risk)

CON:

1. If you get greedy and ignore the warnings, a cold washcloth will be of vital importance.

And that, ladies and gentlemen, concludes the cons. We should also factor in that, according to a 2020 study by Dr. Evan Goldstein, the average American performs or receives oral sex around five times a month.[46] With an average cough drop costing around twenty cents, you'll be getting off pretty cheap. Life's necessities—wine clubs, Netflix, gym memberships, etc.—all add up, so it's wise to be budget conscious. At a yearly cost of only twelve clams, I have a sneaking suspicion this will be the most *fun* and affordable subscription model known to man or woman.

---

[46] *The State of Oral Sex in America*, (Bespoke Surgical, 2020). https://bespokesurgical.com/2020/03/09/oral-sex-in-america/. Article also viewable at: dougfifer.com.

Just when you thought I'd leave you hanging with a surprising statistic, let's backpedal a bit. Americans perform or receive oral sex five times a month? I certainly do not profess to be a mathematician, but I'm guessing most of us are coming up a little short on our monthly allotment. Since blowdrops and mathematics have now collided, however, perhaps cough drop companies could help us out a little by reimagining their marketing campaigns moving forward. After all, a dual-purpose product is always better for consumers. They should capitalize on some of the following trendsetting jingles:

Got a cough, or . . . just need to get off?

Sore throat? Try floating someone's boat.

Throat tickles? Find the pickle.

Throat in pain? Do not abstain.

Nose a little clogged? Time to get those tonsils flogged.

I'm spitballing a few ideas here, but you get the point.

We've always known oral sex is good; we now know it can be better. We've learned that our fellow Americans, on average, get it five times monthly. While average typically sucks, in this case, it sounds pretty darn good. I think the number five is represented perfectly in this equation. When we celebrate something, we often say, "Give me five!" Only, instead of just slapping the hand, it's now within the realm of possibility to pick out your favorite cough drop brand and ask for your one of five for the month. What's the best way to get this slightly salacious journey to utopia green lighted?

Teachable Tidbit: You buy some cough drops, ask your lover for a high five, and then remind them, "Teamwork makes the *dream work.*"

A Gummy Bear Affair . . .

The phrase "doing time" is thought to have been coined in the U.S. when the first prison system was established in 1891. I can't imagine having my personal freedom taken away, and it's incredible to think that the U.S. is the world's leader in incarceration, with an estimated two million people doing time right now.

For those on lockdown, the need for sex doesn't go away. Remember: men think about sex nineteen times a day, with women thinking about it around ten times a day. This book has taught you about prison prostitution, a fuckable taboo tattoo, and prison wolves. So, we know that getting some behind bars is a very real option. But what if you prefer not to tap into any of those choices? Well, that's where jailhouse ingenuity comes in.

In Anchorage, we have a correctional facility that houses only female inmates. From time to time, I would visit the complex to interview a prisoner about a case. Male officers get catcalled in female prisons. It doesn't have anything to do with the cop's looks; he could be butt ugly and overweight, and it wouldn't matter. Was I ever offended by it? Not a chance—who doesn't like being asked to bump uglies now and again?

Correctional officers (COs) in Alaska work the jails and are categorized differently than sworn police officers, but cops and COs all love to shoot the shit and share stories. I remember a CO yelling down the hallway, "Hey, Fifer, you gotta come see this." Correctional officers, like cops, don't just throw out the "gotta see this" over nothing. As I walked into his office, the CO quickly handed me something. Without thinking, I grabbed it before realizing exactly what it was. The CO started laughing his ass off at my expense—I was holding a giant gummy-bear dildo. Cops grab nasty things all the time, but it's usually with latex gloves on. No such luck this time: my hands were barebacking it. I hesitantly asked the CO, "Please tell me this hasn't been used?" He smiled widely and replied, "It's been used and abused." I instantly tossed it onto his desk while throwing out a few choice words.

Where did this supersized sex toy come from? Prisons have commissaries, or jail stores, that allow inmates to purchase stuff. These might include hygiene products, food items, or writing materials, but definitely not dildos. Friends and family typically deposit money into a prisoner's account; otherwise, the prisoners are out of luck. On a side note, can you guess what is the number one purchased item overall in prisons? Believe it or not, it's Ramen noodles. Yup, this tasty treat has replaced cigarettes as the new bartering item of choice.

But back in the day, these female Alaskan prisoners weren't on the Ramen train. They did, however, have a fondness for the sweeter things in life, and sometimes, sweetness and sex go together. So, in the case of the gummy dildo, if it wasn't available for purchase, how did they make it? First, they bought multiple packages of gummy bears from the commissary. Since they don't have Costco sizes in prison, it had to be one small bag at a time. Next, they carefully molded the gummy bears together. But how? They used the prison heating system within the cells. It's cold in Alaska, so the heat is always flowing. To seal the deal, they used a little "prison glue" to coat the finished product. The recipe for this adhesive is simple; mix warm water with powdered coffee creamer and glaze away. Besides holding it together, the coating gives the dildo a glossy and smooth surface. Since the original creator was kind enough to share her invention with other inmates, a sudden explosion in gummy bear sales led to the eventual discovery and subsequent ban of these soft fruit candies.

Teachable Tidbit: Where there's a will, there's a way.

Icebreaker . . .

Do you prefer your cocktails served neat or on the rocks? As for me, I like ice cubes in my drinks. Let me rephrase that: I *once* liked ice cubes. What's my beef with frozen water? Let's just say police work can ruin even the simplest of life's pleasures.

Cops serve search warrants all the time; it's no big deal and part of the job. In straightforward terms, a warrant is a court order from a judge that allows law enforcement to search a person, location, or vehicle for evidence. The number one naughty item found in homes should be no surprise: it's naked pics of the residents. I hate to be too blunt, but these photos usually aren't at the level of Casanova or Miss America. Next up, sex toys abound. Vibrators, dildos, butt plugs, anal beads, pocket pussies, blow-up dolls, and ball gags. A unique one I found rather ridiculous was a fuckable foot. Hear me out—I'm not anti-feet; I just don't get this fetish. We could go on and on debating fuckworthy toys, but let's move on to one of the most shocking discoveries in my twenty-five years of service.

Who would have thought? It was none other than a good ole American ice cube tray. This was some badass technology back in the day, way back in 1844. Jump ahead to 1933, and the first flexible stainless-steel tray is finally invented to eject the cubes. I know what you're thinking: *It took eighty-nine years to figure out this little addition?* What's more, it came with an instruction manual.

You had two options:

1. Twist to remove one ice cube.
2. Twist to remove all the ice cubes.

(These are real directions, people. Let that sink in for a minute.)

What in the world could possibly be so disturbing to me about an ice cube tray? I'm going to let you in on a little secret: truth is stranger than fiction sometimes. This case involved a very influential oil executive. If you didn't know, Alaska has the largest oil field in North America. At 213,543 acres, the Prudhoe Bay oil field is estimated to have originally contained twenty-five billion barrels. This yellowish-black substance is often referred to as "liquid gold." How much does a typical oil tycoon make? This guy was rich—very rich.

Unfortunately for him, however, he was caught up in a brutal divorce. Allegations had been made that he possessed child pornography at his residence. Let's redefine "residence," in this case; it was a mind-bogglingly enormous mansion. *Knock, knock, knock* . . . "This is the Anchorage Police Department with a search warrant. Open the door!" I'm guessing this is an "oh fuck" moment for most criminals—the jig is up. In police work, we assume everyone is lying until we can prove someone is telling the truth. This might sound counterintuitive, but trust is a dangerous path to blindly follow as a cop.

Was this dude a pedophile? Nope—we searched and found nothing. It was later proven to be a false allegation. Yes, the soon-to-be ex-wife was spewing some vitriolic lies. Alaska Statute 11.56.800 criminalizes her behavior, and payback's a bitch. It basically states a person commits the crime of false information or report if the person knowingly gives false information to a peace officer with the intent of implicating another in an offense. I usually don't take joy in slapping on the cuffs, but she was undoubtedly deserving in this case.

Wait! I forgot to discuss the ice cube tray. As it turns out, Mr. Innocent wasn't completely innocent after all. You see, a search warrant allows you to look anywhere that could possibly conceal evidence of a particular crime. In this instance, since child pornography can be contained on a thumb drive, which is small enough to be hidden anywhere, we have complete authority to search everything. Keep in mind that if cops are searching for a stolen TV, for example, they can't open your jewelry box and check out the goods. In the oilman's case, every square inch of his house was a possible hiding spot.

This included the kitchen and even appliances such as the refrigerator. I've never found much in a refrigerator, but I have found drugs and money in the freezer portion. Did I think a hard drive might be hidden behind the ice cream? Not at all. It was more of a check-the-box kind of thing. And sure enough, I found no computer hardware whatsoever. But something else did catch my eye. Stacked neatly together were ice cube trays vacuum packed in plastic bags with specific times and dates written on them. I appreciate fresh ice as much as the next guy, but labeling exactly when it was made seems a bit obsessive-compulsive. Even more curious, it was a Sub-Zero fridge, with a top-of-the-line icemaker. Why have old-fashioned ice trays when you have an icemaker? A few high-end crystal whiskey glasses were also in the freezer, preloaded with ice. While chilling glassware is perfectly normal, prefilling with ice cubes is a no-no. Ice becomes stale over time, and fine whiskey deserves better than that.

The ice in the trays and whiskey glasses looked a little off and not as clear as normal ice. What the heck was it? Could this be some type of synthetic dope? Worse yet, was this creep mixing date rape drugs with ice? If you think it's a little far-fetched, think again. Several cases have been reported where criminals were freezing date rape drugs into ice cubes to avoid detection. Could I legally pull the trays out for inspection? Not really. When you find evidence of another crime—one you are not currently investigating—you're required to stop and modify your search warrant before you can confiscate anything indicating an unrelated crime. If they had been kilos of cocaine, that's exactly what I would have done. But since I didn't know what I had in front of me and didn't presume the husband would lie about it, I went with a more direct approach. I asked him what was in the ice trays. This is my favorite part of police work— when you ask a direct question and then the person repeats the exact question without answering. It's like asking your kid if they finished their homework, and they reply, "Did I finish my homework?"

So, I knew he was stalling when he answered with, "What's in the ice trays?" And I was mentally halfway to the judge's chambers to revise the search warrant. But he quickly followed up with, "Do I have to tell you?" Obviously, he doesn't. I did make clear that without an explanation, I would have another officer stand by the refrigerator, guarding the ice, while I contacted the judge. After that process, we'd likely seize the trays for lab testing. He was adamant that it wasn't dope or anything illegal. Long story short, I convinced him we could all save some time if he just said what it was.

"It's my sperm," he finally answered. The words echoed in my mind *for a minute.* Cops hate to be speechless, but what in the hell was I going to say? The police academy didn't offer Sperm Freezing 101, so if he came up with this lie on the fly, hats off to Ice Boy. Fortunately, he thought it best not to beat around the bush, telling me it was "mostly" for sperm cryopreservation. Before I had a chance to ask him what the hell that was, he said, "It's sperm banking." His doctor had advised him to pursue this option since he was getting older and hadn't had children yet. I couldn't help asking why he was storing it in his freezer. Keep in mind that he was a multimillionaire. He said it was too expensive to store elsewhere, around five hundred bucks a year. Cops love follow-up questions, so next, I asked him why he had *multiple* ice trays filled to the brim. I'll summarize his answer: "If some sperm is good, more is better."

I'm sorry, but jacking off into an ice cube tray on a daily basis seems a little messed up. And good God, how much semen does it take to top off an entire tray? I'm glad you asked. The average male ejaculates between two and four cubic centimeters in volume. A standard ice tray holds one ounce per well, roughly thirty cubic centimeters of water, which means our guy had to masturbate more than 150 times to fill it. If you think back to when I first mentioned this discovery, you will recall I did in fact say *ice trays*—eight in total, each one visibly bagged and tagged. Quick math here estimates somewhere in the range of 1,200 deposits. That number is almost unimaginable! With 365 days in a year, that equates to more than three consecutive years of daily dosing. This dude was obviously good at his job, because he was drilling for oil like nobody's business.

In defense of his forward planning, the thawing survival rate of sperm is somewhere in the vicinity of 50 percent. This would mean around eight hundred of those deposits would never see the light of day. But more importantly, I should mention seminal fluid must be frozen at a constant temperature of negative 196 degrees Celsius. A typical home freezer comes in around negative eighteen degrees Celsius. Bottom line: none of his boys would swim again. Oh yeah—I failed to say what he *actually* meant by "mostly for sperm cryopreservation." Remember those whiskey glasses? Sure enough, they contained 100 percent genetic material. Whatever you do, I wouldn't advise googling the term "cum cube party." As it turned out, my man was part of a swinger's club that indulged in this fetish. I guess sharing *is* caring. I need to apologize for mocking foot fetishes earlier, because I'd gladly fuck a silicone foot all day long before swapping cum cubes with the boys.

How big can cum fetishes really be? Well, at fetishhookups. com, you can pretty much match any sexual fixation, and yes, they offer cum fetish dating, finding like-minded hookups for this peculiar kink. Recently, OnlyFans star Nick Finch filled up a Tupperware container one sperm load at a time for viewers. He collected deposits until he had enough to create a cooking video on YouTube, "Cooking Man Juice Experiment." He bakes some, boils some, fries some, and then eats his own cooked cum. What's even more distasteful, he has over one hundred thousand Instagram followers and nearly the same number of YouTube subscribers. To see his actual "spermathon" video, you'll have to pony up twenty-five dollars a month. If you think nobody's paying for this type of content, keep in mind that OnlyFans top earners are making in excess of $100,000 a month! This begs an unprecedented culinary question: could Nick Finch beat Bobby Flay? If that competition ever happens, I feel bad for the judges during the blind taste test. On the other hand, the meal *would* be low fat; semen only contains around five to twenty-five calories per ejaculation.

For our bonus **Teachable Tidbit**, our semen aficionado exposes two best practices:

First off, have some class by not giving *stale* cum cubes to your swinger friends. Sperm freezes in under two hours, so plan accordingly.

Second, if you want to stock up on semen for future breeding, you'll need to buy a proper liquid-nitrogen cryogenic semen storage system . . . and that tongue twister will set you back a cool eight grand online.

The Crisco Kid . . .

Who doesn't like makeup sex? We've all had those unpleasant arguments that spontaneously turn into a passionate fuck fest. Why is this type of sex more intense than a typical roll in the sack? It seems improbable you can be at each other's throats mere minutes before lustfully ripping clothes off. Dr. Justin Lehmiller, a research fellow at the Kinsey Institute, says that sex relieves stress, "so it stands to reason that makeup sex could help reduce feelings of stress and allow couples to move on faster." The phenomenon is called "excitation transfer," according to Lehmiller. "Basically," he says, "the idea is that if you have carryover arousal from, say, a fight with your partner that you bring into the bedroom, it can make the ensuing sex more intense."[47] Based on this information, I guess makeup sex is worth fighting for.

The following event also relates to anger and sex, but with the intensity kicked up a notch. We're talking about eroticized rage, where the individual uses sex to humiliate, exact revenge,

---

[47] Gigi Engle, *Is Makeup Sex a Good Thing or a Bad Thing for Your Relationship?*, (Men's Health, 2019). https://www.menshealth.com/sex-women/a28747439/makeup-sex/. Article also viewable at: dougfifer.com.

and punish their victims. This behavior includes abnormal sex or fetishes that stand outside of social norms. The bottom line of this story: your version of fighting and fucking probably isn't so bad after all. The following message from our dispatch center is how it all began:

> "We have a report of a vehicle, a dark-colored Ford truck, parked on private property. The complainant advised they watched it pull in about an hour prior. They can see a lot of movement inside of the vehicle but can't tell what's going on."

At the time, I was 99 percent sure we had two people fucking in a truck. As you'll soon find out, however, God bless that other 1 percent! It truly keeps things interesting. On this wintry day, I was working day-shift hours, which, at this time of year in southern Alaska, meant only a few hours of daylight. If you didn't know, Anchorage only receives about five hours of sunlight on the day of winter solstice. Now, I'm not complaining because it could be worse; the residents of Utqiaġvik, Alaska's northernmost town, don't see the sun for nearly two months. In other words, the sun sets in November and doesn't rise again until January. But even Utqiaġvik's never-ending night can't hold a candle to the following individual's darkness.

Police protocol sends two cops to check out situations like this. We typically resolve it quickly by telling the lovebirds to move along and find somewhere else to screw. Before approaching the truck, we parked our cop cars at the end of a long driveway, which led to an open and undeveloped lot. Having not been regularly plowed, the area was covered in snow. We walked in on foot for a couple of reasons. The first had to do with safety; being on foot gave us the advantage with the element of surprise. The second equally important reason was to avoid getting our cars stuck in the snow.

As we walked in, we followed one of the tire impressions made by the vehicle. This kept us from having to wade through a few feet of snow. Four by four trucks easily traverse winter conditions, and for that reason, they are a favorite mode of transportation in Alaska. Unfortunately for cops, cities and states have limited budgets, so we tend to get the cheaper vehicles without the option of four-wheel drive. No biggie—being an Alaskan cop means we must trudge through snow from time to time. The officer with me was an old-timer; he was no-nonsense when it came to police work. He stood about six feet and four inches tall, and he was built like a brick shithouse. He took the lead and told me, "Let's just tell them to get the hell out of here." I wasn't going to argue; besides being a bit intimidating, he was also right.

About halfway to the truck, which was facing away from us, a young male jumped out of the driver's side. He started walking quickly toward us saying that everything was okay. We met up about a hundred feet from the truck. I was directly behind the other officer, trying to stay in the tire track. I leaned a bit to the side so I could keep an eye on the male. It probably wasn't the safest approach, but deep snow is like lava to cops. It's annoying when your boots and pants get wet, so we avoid it at all costs. The young male was no different, so imagine the three of us standing in a line along a tire impression that was less than two feet wide.

The senior officer asked him what he was doing parked there for so long. His quick answer of "nothing" wasn't good enough; it usually isn't. My partner's follow-up question didn't fare any better. When he asked the young male who else was in the vehicle, he said, "Nobody." As a result, we had nothing and nobody to go on. If I only had a nickel for every time a criminal told me these exact two words. The truck's back window was fogged up, a good indication that sex had been in play. My partner repeated his questions. Receiving the exact same answers, he took matters into his own hands.

He went to step around the male and check on the other occupant of the truck. Really, all we were looking for was two consenting adults. When that happens, it's as easy as them leaving and us leaving. But here is where it got complicated. As the other officer tried to move past, the male grabbed his arm. This is the number one no-no for interactions with cops—we truly take offense at being grabbed. Citizens normally don't do that, so we can only assume in those moments that you're either half crazed or attempting to hurt us. It's hard for us to guess. Consequently, we are left with little choice but to act. In this case, before I could respond, the male was already on the ground being handcuffed. Remember when I said my partner could be intimidating? Well, this young man might as well have picked a fight with Dwayne "The Rock" Johnson. It was game over before it even started.

As my fellow officer stood up, I could see something wasn't right. His eyes widened, and he had a puzzled look on his face. For a split second, my heart nearly stopped as I anxiously asked him if he was okay. It wouldn't be the first time an officer was injured or stabbed during a seemingly uneventful takedown. I thanked God when he said he wasn't hurt, but he quickly followed up with, "What the fuck is on my arm!" He raised his right arm toward me, and I could see some type of clear, thick substance on it. Being a bit confused, I could only repeat his words: "What the fuck is that?"

Before I could say anything else, he bent down and shouted at our handcuffed guy sitting in the snow, "You better tell me what's all over my goddamn arm." The good news was that his answer this time wasn't "nothing" or "nobody." The bad news was that it was still a typical criminal answer, "I don't know." I can't tell you the number of times I've pulled drugs out of a suspect's pockets, asked them what it was, and received the answer, "I don't know." Before the cop, a.k.a. The Rock, had a chance to tear this guy's head off, I intervened. I refocused his energy and reminded him we still had someone else in the truck. Without another word, he turned and stomped off toward the vehicle.

I stayed with the handcuffed guy and told him, "Don't even think about moving." The driver's side door of the truck was still wide open. I watched intently as my partner walked up. The call had elevated slightly in tension after the sudden hands-on inter-action. I wasn't sure what he'd find. I remember him drawing his firearm as he approached the open door. At that moment, I pulled my own gun out, thinking he had spotted something. After looking in, he quickly looked back toward me. It was round two of that wide-eyed and puzzled look. After a few shakes of his head, he holstered his firearm. I recall thinking that we were back to our original 99 percent probability of just two people fooling around.

The odd thing was that the officer started walking back toward me. If someone else was in the vehicle, he wouldn't simply turn his back and walk away. As he got closer to us, he said, "Hey, dumbass," at which point I wondered if he was going to start yelling at our suspect again. Only, the "dumbass" was intended for me, followed up with "Put your gun away." *Shit*, I thought. I felt like an idiot. Not missing a beat, he leaned over to our guy and said, "You've got some explaining to do, you sick fuck." I asked him what was going on in the truck. With a grimace on his face, my partner blurted out, "Go take a look for yourself."

I marched right up to the driver's side door in anticipation of something good. When cops say, "Look for yourself," it's usually a rude awakening. At first glance, I didn't even know what I was looking at. The truck was an older model with a bench seat. On the seat were several items: a magazine, a large butcher knife, a can of Crisco, and an empty box of tissues. A closer inspection of the magazine, which appeared to be torn up, was a "holy fuck" moment for me. It was a porn magazine featuring completely nude females in various positions. The pages had been slashed repeatedly using the butcher knife. The Crisco—here it comes—was the lube for beating off while stabbing the naked women.

Again, when I say the 1 percent keeps it interesting, I mean it. Cops live for this exact type of call. "The sicker, the better" is our motto. Does police work warp you a bit? Probably so, but society sure isn't helping to restore us to normalcy.

What happened to the Crisco Kid? Well, that has been my question for the last twenty years. First off, masturbating alone in your vehicle in a secluded area is not a crime. Violently stabbing a porn magazine, again, is not a crime. Using Crisco instead of . . . let's say . . . lotion—it's not a crime. Emptying an entire box of tissues while thinking about a violent sexual act? Nope, still not a crime. Grabbing a cop? Now, that's getting closer, but we didn't charge him. The guy, really a kid, was only nineteen years old. He didn't have any prior criminal history, no open cases—he wasn't even a blip on our radar. What about the cop's arm? Yeah, that was Crisco all the way. Hopefully, it wasn't intermixed with any bodily fluids. My partner, by this time, was very concerned with getting the vegetable shortening off his arm. Feeling the need to be supportive, I told him to just grab a tissue from the truck. It seemed convenient since the floorboard was littered with wadded-up Kleenex.

Are you wondering if we simply let this predator in the making go? My answer would be "yes and no." At that very moment, without any charges, we had to let him go. As far as preventing the 99 percent chance of the Crisco Kid committing future crimes, I had a plan. I asked the department if we could form a team, almost like a task force, to track individuals like these. I thought that since they were almost certainly going to rape, pillage, and plunder, we should stop them before it starts. We were sworn to protect and to serve, so let's get to it. I hadn't quite considered the number of man hours, civil liberty violations, and people out there who are just like the Crisco Kid. You could task every cop in every department across our nation to track one sick fuck 24-7, and the sad reality is that you'd run out of cops.

I can tell you, nevertheless, I kept my eyes and ears out for this guy for many years. I never saw his name come across the wants and warrants list, police reports, or as a suspect of a violent crime. To this day, I have no idea what happened to the Crisco Kid. It still haunts me a bit, as his behavior seemed to me to be the start of something more sinister. Fantasizing about homicidal behavior while sexually gratifying yourself is borderline sociopathic. He'd be nearing his forties about now. Is he in prison, dead, or actively wreaking havoc on society? Okay, I purposefully left out the "productive citizen" option, because I personally don't believe there is a chance in hell.

As a hostage negotiator, I was trained in the art of profiling individuals during critical situations. This version of profiling was not in the traditional sense of creating one that would assist in a future apprehension. Negotiators are in the moment, talking live with criminals to obtain insights into their current motives and actions. We can then use this information to facilitate a surrender. The FBI has a Behavioral Analysis Unit where agents can create a profile of an unknown perpetrator based on a specific set of circumstances. They can predict psychological traits as well as behavioral tendencies. In the simplest of terms, criminal profiling is a cross between law enforcement and psychology.

Does it work? Remember the necrophiliac serial killer Ted Bundy? His final capture was attributed, in part, to this behavioral science. After confessing to thirty murders (but suspected of more than a hundred), Bundy was put to death in the electric chair. Before being sent to hell, however, he reached out to law enforcement while on death row. At the time, recent news stories on the Green River Killer had piqued Bundy's interest. He wanted to help investigators get inside the mind of an uncaptured serial killer. And guess what? Authorities agreed. I mean, who better to profile a serial killer than another serial killer?

Imagine what an FBI criminal profiler would say about the Crisco Kid. Did his mommy not love him enough? Did he wet the bed, torture animals, or get bullied in school? I've always wanted to know, and I bet you do too. What could have created this behavior, and what makes this guy tick? How about we find out together? Through my contacts in law enforcement, I requested a behavioral study and profile on the Crisco Kid. FBI Supervisory Special Agent Leonard Opanashuk, now retired, is a certified profiler and former prosecutor with over twenty-five years of experience investigating, prosecuting, analyzing, researching, consulting, and instructing on violent crimes against adult and child victims. He's worked some of America's toughest cases, so let's see what he thinks about this one.

A. Case Facts

Police responded to a call for a dark-colored Ford truck parked on private property during daylight hours. The complaining witness indicated there was a lot of movement happening in the truck. The truck was further described as an older model, "beater" type vehicle.

The vehicle was parked in a large, undeveloped lot with a long driveway. It was snow covered, and the snow level necessitated the officers approach the vehicle on foot. The officers' suspicion was that people were in the parked truck having sex.

When the officers were halfway to the truck, a male individual, hereafter "Crisco Kid," exited the vehicle and quickly approached the officers while telling them that everything was okay. The officers asked Crisco Kid what he was doing, and his response was "Nothing." They then asked who he was with, and the response was "Nobody." The truck's windows were steamed up, which suggested to the officers that someone else was inside.

As the first officer attempted to move past Crisco Kid, Crisco Kid grabbed the officer's arm, which resulted in Crisco Kid being placed in handcuffs. As the officer completed handcuffing Crisco Kid, he became aware of an unknown substance that transferred from Crisco Kid's hand to his arm. Demands to know what was on the officer's arm were answered with "I don't know."

When officers inspected the interior of the vehicle, they located a container of Crisco, an empty box of tissues, a butcher knife, and a pornographic magazine depicting females in a variety of positions, which had been stabbed and cut with the knife. The tissues from the box were scattered about the floor of the truck.

Crisco Kid had been masturbating in his truck while stabbing and slashing the women in the pornographic magazine.

Crisco Kid is described as a tall, thin, white male, nineteen years of age. He lived alone with his mother and was both unemployed and a high school dropout. He indicated that he never had a girlfriend and that stabbing and slashing the magazine while masturbating excited him. He stated that he did not want to harm women. He was further described as meek and avoided direct eye contact with the officers. The officers assessed that he had limited intelligence.

B. Analysis

The question posed here is what the potential trajectory of Crisco Kid is, given the known behavior described above. While it is difficult to predict outcomes with specificity considering the limited facts presented in this case, the behavior and possible trajectory can be discussed in general terms.

Crisco Kid took certain steps to conceal his activity, showing that he was cognizant of others' possible disapproval or even possible legal consequences resulting from his behavior. He did not engage in this activity in his home, presumably to avoid discovery by his mother. When the officers first approached, he attempted to mitigate the discovery by engaging with officers outside of his vehicle. He tried to avoid discovery by going so far as grabbing an officer's arm to prevent or dissuade him from going any further.

People who engage in sexually deviant behavior are sexually aroused by images, fantasies, and acts that would be considered socially unacceptable or illegal, so they may take extra steps to conceal their activities out of fear of the possible consequences.

In this instance, Crisco Kid took steps to conceal his activity by leaving his home and driving to a remote spot so he would not be discovered and potentially suffer consequences for his behavior. Additionally, he was likely aware that his behavior would be concerning to police, and he attempted to mitigate that by his actions and his words, including telling the police that he did not want to hurt women.

Crisco Kid's sexual deviance is the result of the fusion of sex and violence in his fantasy. Offenders who eventually commit sexual homicide obtain sexual gratification from the violence of the homicide itself. At some point in their early lives, sexual gratification and violence become fused together in their fantasies. This happens in a variety of ways, including early childhood abuse, witnessing sexually violent acts, or exposure to sexually violent pornography. Without clinical intervention to untangle this fusion, the outcome can lead to sexual assault and murder. Fantasy is sometimes a substitute for action, but it can also be the preparation for action. The more Crisco Kid engages in this behavior, the greater the likelihood he will try to act on it.

In the background of sexual homicide offenders, there is commonly found a criminal history of "behavioral tryouts." These are cases where the offender is inching closer to action by engaging in activities like peeping, exposure, casing homes, stalking, or breaking and entering. Although the real reason remains sexual, often the law only captures these incidents as generic disorderly conduct, loitering, indecent exposure, harassment, trespass, or burglary offenses. Sometimes intervention in these "behavioral tryouts" by law enforcement is the only thing that prevents further action. As an offender increasingly engages in these activities, they become more adept, confident, and prepared.

C. Conclusion

An individual who has sexually violent fantasies, like Crisco Kid, may not act on them for many years or at all. For Crisco Kid, there could be many interventions, clinical or otherwise, over the course of his life that change his trajectory for the better or maybe for the worse. These other interventions could be a stabilizing force in his life, like a girlfriend or spouse, job, or school. The intervention could also come from law enforcement action.

Given the limited facts, it is difficult to predict a specific outcome in this case. Crisco Kid's behavior is certainly a big red flag that requires clinical intervention.

That we don't know what happened to him could mean an intervention took place, he ended up in prison for a behavioral tryout, sexual offense, or worse, or he suffered an untimely death before he could act any further. He could still be out there waiting for the right opportunity. [48]

Teachable Tidbit: If by chance you run out of traditional sexual lubrications, you now have two options. Grab some Crisco to bake some bread or use it to jack off instead.

[48] The observations, opinions, and suggestions contained herein are the result of the knowledge drawn from personal investigative experience, educational background, specialized training, and research. This analysis is not a substitute for a thorough and well-planned investigation and should not be considered all inclusive. The information provided is based on probabilities. The offender may not fit the analysis in every aspect.

CONCLUSION

Wrapping up this book is like putting a condom on after sex; you've already been fucked, so what's the point? The point is that most of us still want to get a bit freakier while fucking. The dilemma arises when our innermost sexual desires overpower our moral principles. Is what we crave natural or deviant? Well, it certainly depends on how you fulfill your fetish. I have a sneaking suspicion your game is rather lame—that is, compared to the sins within these pages. But to verify, I have a simple review that might help.

Let's take this time to cover the "shoulds" and "shouldn'ts" of sex. Name That Crime taught us that fucking Fido is frowned upon, whereas a giant cucumber up one's ass might be perfectly okay—just don't drive drunk while you're doing it. Tossing semen is a no-no without the express consent of the receiving individual. For the male perpetrators out there, we should confirm that consent doesn't simply mean standing in the same aisle at a Walmart. Being a Playboy Playmate, a.k.a. "Bad Bunny," sounds sexy as hell, but finding sexual pleasure in killing people (i.e., erotophonophilia) falls within the "shouldn't" category.

"Kink and Ink" covered the history of tattooing while providing several valuable lessons. We learned that a mummy fetish involving Ötzi the Iceman really does exist. We established that do-it-yourself dick and ball tattoos generally turn out badly. We discovered an unstoppable force known as heroin, which destructively alters lives forever. We saw firsthand how the Mexican Mafia exploits the use of this drug to exert control over its criminal organization. We won't soon forget the term "prison wolf"—being straight on the outside but gay on the inside. Or how the Mexican Mafia strictly prohibits gang members from homosexual sex, unless, of course, your male partner has a beautiful woman tattooed on his backside. You might want to think about the plight of a man with a tattoo like this whenever you are having a bad day or feeling a little down; perhaps a little perspective is necessary. By perspective, I mean a big fat reality check, because you've probably never been pimped out strictly due to a back tat. So, on those gloomy days, go back to chapter three and remember: it's not so bad after all.

"Makin' Bacon" truly defines our insatiable love of pork, but can this love go too far? It can when you go to a barn in order to buttfuck a pig and wallow in the animal's poo while wearing a T-shirt that reads "Dirty Old Man." When in doubt, it's important to follow this simple guide:

Should I eat bacon? Yes.

Should I fuck bacon? No.

If you're into dicks and fondly call your partner "Big Dick," it's probably a win for you both. But this changes dramatically when your partner is a horse with a twenty-four to thirty-two-inch erect penis. Enticing a stallion to painfully fuck you to death falls soundly into the "shouldn't" category.

Ninety-three percent of us order a pizza at least once a month. Hands down, it's America's favorite comfort food. Should I put away a few slices of pizza pie from time to time? Absolutely. Should I blow my load all over it and then masturbate again knowing others are eating it? Clearly this one moves into the "shouldn't" classification. When in doubt, you should always hold the anchovies.

Fucking anything dead is invariably going to jump into the "shouldn't" region. It doesn't matter if it's man or beast. Zero exceptions here—sorry, moose molesters and serial killers; it's a no-go for all. Oh yeah, forgive me, ladies; you can't bang yourself with someone's dead bones either. To summarize, cracking open a cold one is for beer only.

"The Last Climax" neatly clarifies the "shouldn'ts" of sex. We learned that when autoerotic asphyxiation goes bad, it goes really bad. "The Professor's Last Lesson" taught us that Mozart, gas masks, giant dildos, and Amsterdam Poppers can be a deadly combo. Remembering "Bob the Builder" will make you think twice about your unsuspecting neighbors. What anal-play scenarios might they be into? The best case is hopefully just anal beads, while the worst case is skewering themselves to death with a large metal object. And as for edible kinks, who knew Cheez Whiz wasn't just for snacks? Product directions recommend holding the applicator tip close to the food while pressing firmly and moving slowly across the surface. They might want to add the following direction for alternate uses: "Insert the applicator tip into the anus while pressing firmly until the cavity is filled." The "contents under pressure" warning might need some updating as well. For example—"Caution: not recommended for three-way sex contracts, wet suits, or any form of total enclosure fetishism."

We discovered that being autosexual, or loving yourself and yourself alone, doesn't necessarily equate to safe sex. The man in the mirror kept his eye on the prize all the way to his demise. He got a *little* too frisky with the leotard, mittens, duct tape, and rope. Although tragic, they say true love is defined by loving someone until your last breath, so at least he had that going for him. Last but certainly not least, "Riding Harleys and Hoovers" shed light on the underground world of the Hells Angels. Okay, maybe not entirely, but it did get to the bottom of a top-level member riding more than just his Harley.

Now on to some "shoulds." My Teachable Tidbits are a safe and legal way to expand your sexual desires. The oracle provided us with a recipe for taking oral sex to the next level. If it already feels amazing and can be leveled up, it's a no-brainer. Just remember not to get greedy—use only one cough drop at a time. Also, ladies, if by chance you ever find yourself doing hard time without a vibrator, simply visit the prison commissary for some gummy bears and coffee creamer. Life is all about having the tools necessary to succeed.

Cumming into ice cube trays, in all honesty, is an odd one for me. I'll pass on the cum cube parties, but to each their own. If you are going to cryogenically preserve your sperm, keep in mind that home freezers won't work. If that's your thing, then buying a proper nitrogen freezer is a "should." How about Crisco for beating off? Maybe. As for stabbing naked women in a porn magazine with a giant butcher knife? Sorry, Crisco Kid—this is a clear overstep and belongs under the "shouldn't" column.

In the end, we've quoted Shakespeare, noted Mozart, laid eyes on Leonardo da Vinci's finest painting, and explored history together, combining the highs and lows of culture, art, and fucking. I hope this has been a thought-provoking journey, my friends, but before we part ways, I have one more thing to say:

Your sex life is perfectly normal, so for God's sake, go ahead and fuck with the lights on!

ABOUT THE AUTHOR

Doug Fifer is a retired Alaskan police officer who specialized in crime scene analysis, deviant sexual crimes, hostage
negotiations, and various special assignments throughout his
twenty-five-year career. He started in law enforcement with the
Anchorage Police Department in 1996 and retired in 2021.

Born in the small town of Homer, Alaska, Doug and his wife,
Kim, raised their children in the Anchorage area. His family originates from southeast Alaska, mainly around the Ketchikan area.
He is Tlingit Indian and heavily connected to his Alaska Native
culture and heritage.

Doug and Kim are also avid oenophiles who started a wine
business in Anchorage in 2007. Alaskans have a passionate love
for the outdoors, and the Fifer family is no exception. Fishing,

hiking, snowboarding, and extreme sports top their list. Their family dog, Malbec, is considered one of the kids and snowboards a bit too.

As the author of *Fifty Shades of True Crime*, Doug brings to life stories so bizarre, so intense, and so twisted that the reader will be left speechless. This is not your run-of-the-mill true crime; it's straight from the source, an author-led journey into how far some will go to achieve their sexually freakish desires. As a highly decorated investigator, Doug has negotiated with serial killers, solved homicides, and worked real-life cases that will shock you to the core. You've never read a book quite like this one; it's a cringeworthy reality check on humanity. You might think you can handle the truth, but this cop's truth is as savage as it gets.

When asked about the stressors of being a cop, Doug replied, "Humor plays a key role in keeping your sanity, not just in law enforcement but life in general." His writing certainly reflects this philosophy, as Doug believes in taking life seriously—just not too seriously.

An updated and expanded list of resources for *Fifty Shades of True Crime* is available at dougfifer.com.

Want more true crime? Sign up for advance notice of new books by this author.